HELLO,
Young Mothers

*A Peek Behind the
Motherhood Curtain*

By

CAREEN STRANGE

To Burt Sr.

my perfect Lead Man

He who fears the Lord has a secure fortress,
and for his children it will be a refuge.
Proverbs 14:26 (NIV)

CONTENTS

A Word From the Author....................................vii
Meet the Cast ix
Prologue.. xi

ACT I: THE CHILDHOOD STAGE.....................15
Scene One: Party of One
Scene Two: Now You See Him...
Scene Three: Epiphany
Scene Four: New Pecking Order
Scene Five: Needing Daddy
Scene Six: Saturday Sabbath
Scene Seven: Perfect Seven
Scene Eight: Messing Around
Scene Nine: Strange Family Vacation

ACT II: THE BOYHOOD STAGE.......................55
Scene One: School Days Begin
Scene Two: Boys Mature (or Not)
Scene Three: Being Spontaneous
Scene Four: The Walk
Scene Five: Boys Mature (Really)
Scene Six: Chores
Scene Seven: Shop 'Till You Drop
Scene Eight: Individual Time
Scene Nine: Discipline
Scene Ten: Day Off

Scene Eleven: Bumps, Bruises, and Worse
Scene Twelve: School Morning
Scene Thirteen: Redneck Fishin' Boat
Scene Fourteen: Perfect Mother
Scene Fifteen: Season of Life
Scene Sixteen: Christmas at Our House

ACT III: THE TEEN STAGE 119
Scene One: Changes
Scene Two: Making Friends With Friends
Scene Three: Getting to Know You
Scene Four: Basketball Camp
Scene Five: Sex Ed
Scene Six: Different Beach Scene
Scene Seven: Home for Boys
Scene Eight: Life is Beautiful
Scene Nine: A Mother's Heart

CURTAIN CALL 151

A WORD FROM THE AUTHOR

Don't let me confuse you. This is not a play; it is a book. It is the very intimate and personal story of my adventures in motherhood as my husband and I were bringing up our five sons.

I use a stage play as a metaphor. (That's what happens when you're a retired drama teacher.) This book is divided into three sections, which I call Acts, and instead of chapters, I refer to them as scenes. These scenes are excerpts taken directly from journals I kept when the boys were growing up, followed by my comments written now that our sons have become adults. The episodes cover a span of approximately eighteen years as the boys transitioned from toddlers into high school gradu-ates. The dates of the journal entries aren't always in chrono-logical order because I arranged them according to the subject of what I wanted to share.

I'm the so-called Director. Our family members are the characters and at the end there is a Curtain Call when our now-adult sons introduce themselves and say what they wish to say. I wrote this book not as a professional or as an experi-enced writer, but as a woman who had on-the-job, crash course training in motherhood. When I began this project I thought it would be as a memoir for my family, but now I'm sharing it in faith that it will help women who are in the throes of child rearing. By depicting life as it was for me, sharing some of the delights I had and the lessons I learned as our boys were growing up, I hope to come alongside younger women to coach and encourage them. I have visions of some young mom hugging my book to her chest exclaiming, "Yes! I love this woman! She understands me, and I now have hope!"

Frankly, I struggled with the challenges of bringing up our small clan. One minute I could feel such a love for my children my chest hurt, and the next minute I was clenching my fist. Guilt overwhelmed me when I realized I was enduring rather than enjoying my blessings. There has never been anything in my life that could come close to the joy I had mothering our boys, but to be honest, some days were miserable!

I am a successful mother for one reason: I allowed Jesus Christ to be Lord of my life, and I trusted His Holy Spirit to guide me as I reared our children. I pray you will be entertained, encouraged, and inspired in your motherhood journey, but more than anything I pray you will realize, as I have, that God the Father was the producer, Jesus Christ was the divine Director, and the Holy Spirit was the infallible prompter behind the curtain.

Careen Strange
2014

MEET THE CAST

The Parents:

Careen and Burt Strange Sr. are the Mom and Dad in this show. Careen also speaks as the Director. Together they have experienced the disciplines and the delights of forty-four years of marriage. Each year finds them loving each other more and enjoying the companionship of their growing family, comprised of five sons, three daughters-in-law, and eight grandchildren, age six and younger. They also enjoy having an occasional quiet house.

The Boys:

There are five boys, with a nine-year age span from oldest to youngest: Burt Jr., Adam, Jed, Clint, and Josh. Despite the boisterous atmosphere of their developing years, they all emerged safely into adulthood. They are a diverse mixture of temperaments, talents, and tastes. They are all competitive, entrepreneurial, opinionated, and ambitious. Yet they also are perceptive, compassionate, and honoring to God, to their parents, and to each other (now). And they all love their mama.

The Grandparents:

Affectionately known as Papa, JoJo, and Gran (Granddaddy already in heaven), these were the best grandparents any boys could have, always willing to lend a helping hand and relieve Mom and Dad. Because the boys were the only grandchildren on both sides of the family, they received all the love, all the attention, and all the instructive opportunities offered by the older generation. The grandparents played a huge role in the development of the boys' character. They left a legacy of godliness and wonderful memories for their posterity.

The Backstage Crew:

This group includes babysitters and housekeepers, too numerous to name everyone. Though the boys had uncontested devotion from both parents, Mom and Dad also made time for their own relationship to flourish. The babysitting pool consisted of girls from Mom's Sunday School class and older teens from the youth group that met in our home. The boys enjoyed these girls and guys—only they preferred calling them man-sitters instead of babysitters.

Emma was the longest tenured housekeeper. Having thirteen children of her own, she came to Mom when the first son was born, and showed her how to take care of a newborn. For more than twenty years, four days a week, the family benefitted from Emma's wisdom and experience. One of the younger boys told his kindergarten teacher he had a stepmother and her name was Emma.

PROLOGUE

Imagine a theater. Lights dimmed. The curtain rises on a kaleidoscope of action: actresses laden with infant carriers, diaper bags, and bulging purses are traversing the stage. They're propelling strollers, pushing shopping carts, and coercing children. Over sounds of babies crying, toddlers whining, children laughing, teens yelling, and siblings squabbling, the show's theme song competes for attention. It's a takeoff of the song "Hello Young Lovers," from the Broadway musical *The King and I.*

Hello Young Mothers

Hello, Young mothers, whoever you are,
I hope your troubles are few.
All my good wishes are with you just now;
I've been a mom like you.

Be strong, young mothers, and follow your heart,
Be strong, dedicated, and true.
The task you've been given is worth all the pain;
I've been a mom like you.

I know how it feels to have kids on your heels
And fly through the day in a trance.
You run here and there, and you're hardly aware of the
Time between soccer and dance.

So cry, young mothers, if you feel that you must,
But don't cry that you're not alone.
Cry for the days that will pass in a blur
When you find that your children are grown.

All of my memories are happy today,
But I've had those times of my own.

Be brave, young mothers, and follow your heart,
Be brave, devoted, and true.
Cling very close to your children tonight;
I've been a mom like you.

I know how it feels to cringe at the squeals
And to hope that your feelings don't show,
To yearn for a date and a chance to escape
With the lover that you used to know.

Take heart, young mothers, whatever you do,
Don't cry that you're not alone.
All of your memories will be happy one day;
You'll smile at the days that are gone.

~Careen Strange
2004

With that introduction, let's open the curtains and reveal the scenes. But first, here's a preview of what's to come…

December 13, 1982
Dear Journal,

It's a perfect morning for sleeping. The bedroom is cool and I've found the warm cozy spot as I snuggle under the covers. There is just enough weight at my left side to give me something to nestle against. The smell of coffee comes wafting by me, and the sound of a bird's cheeping is somewhere in the nether land of my dreams. It's a late fall morning…I hear the sound of a pick-up truck cranking. I stretch.

As I force my arm over my head I realize how cold the room actually is and I gradually start to recognize what I don't hear is the usual heat pump noise. I also am becoming aware that I can't roll over because the weight pressing next to me is a very wet- diapered three-year-old who is trying to get warm. Reality overtakes me as I see the insistent cheeping is coming from the alarm that is set for 4:45 a.m., and the one responsible for that is driving off in his truck, headed to his deer stand. Furthermore, the reason for the chill is because the heat is not working.

I'm almost coherent as I struggle against the weight of the covers and the sleeping bundle resting against me and brace myself for the draft of cold air that is going to hit me as I rise to slap the alarm into silence. At that moment I almost stumble and fall over the two sleeping children who have managed to sneak into our bedroom sometime in the night and set up camp on the floor beside our bed. The six-year-old and the four-year-old are almost indistinguishable from the mound of stuffed animals that are piled around their heads as they slumber in contentment.

The rest of the morning rolls over me like a tsunami. Bowls and glasses are everywhere, a pile of hunting gear is in the corner, binoculars, flashlights, caps, and gloves are covering the kitchen counter — and suddenly it's lunchtime and everybody is hungry again! Thankfully, I have (for once) done something ahead of time, and I pull from the refrigerator the pot of chili made the day before. By the time this meal is finished, there is not a single clean bowl left. There are empty glasses left on the table, which is covered with saltine cracker crumbs. Of course the guys don't notice because the next order of events is to hurry to the dove field for a bird shoot.

I stand at the window and watch them, dressed in camouflage from head to toe, as they pile in the back of their dad's pick-up truck, laughing and joking with each other. By this time, there are a few other dads and sons who have congregated in our front yard, and they leave together. The younger boys have elected to stay at home and play, content to have the basketball goal and the yard to themselves without the interference of the older ones. I return to the kitchen to address the disaster left in the wake of their invasion.

Cleanup complete, I'm finally able to collapse in front of the fire and enjoy a few moments without interruption. Sitting here, I hear the sound of happy, healthy children: the thump of the basketball, the grinding of riding toys' sandy tires on the concrete driveway, and the pounding of feet chasing each other around the outside of the house.

I know it won't always be like this: a blend of mud-caked boots at the front door, footballs scattered on the lawn, strewn towels left from half-washed hands, shotgun shells scattered on the floor, shotgun pellets in the carpet, sometimes runny noses and wet beds, but always spontaneous hugs and aura of contentment.

I'll miss this one day...

ACT I

THE CHILDHOOD STAGE

Children are a gift from the Lord; they are a reward from
Him. Children born to a young man are like sharp arrows in
a warrior's hands. How happy is the man whose
quiver is full of them!
Psalm 127:3-5 (NLT)

SCENE ONE: PARTY OF ONE

December 1, 1979
Dear Journal,

Today I had a party. For myself. Just me. Nobody came and I didn't care. I feel like nobody knows I exist. There were breakfast dishes on the table, globs of oatmeal on the chairs, Legos scattered over the floor, and dirty laundry everywhere. I didn't put on any makeup and my hair is out of style. I don't even know what style is anymore.

At one time, this wasn't true. I can remember when I loved my life. I was being creative, and using my talents, and I felt...what? Purposeful, that's it. Just now I feel like the world is passing by, and I will live and die and no one will ever know I was ever here.

To make matters worse, I feel so guilty that I can't stand to look in the mirror. I have five beautiful, healthy children that God has blessed me with, but I feel like I can't do anything for Him because of them. They need me every minute.

On days like this my mind flashed back to an episode that took place ten years earlier. The event happened in the modest cabin Burt and I had transformed from a dismal faded green exterior to chocolate-red with white trim — the love-nest for our new life together. Built as a stay for weekend deer hunters, our little house was situated in the midst of a thick planting of Georgia pine trees and seemed isolated from the world. After a short three months of married life, the feeling of isolation was even more pronounced when I found myself pregnant with our first child before I'd time to make a single new friend in the rural South Georgia town where we lived.

I didn't feel well for several weeks, but not knowing how a pregnant person was supposed to feel, I ignored it. That is, until my doctor examined me and said the placenta had begun to separate from my uterus and I would probably abort the baby. "Don't worry about it," he said. "You're healthy and you will certainly have more pregnancies. Just call me if you have a problem."

That night I had a problem.

It was early December. I had spent the afternoon decorating our little place for Christmas: two large and one tiny stocking hung on the wagon wheel over the fireplace. That was about it. I didn't have the energy or the materials to do much else. At 3:00 a.m. I woke up aware something was wrong. I was hemorrhaging. I woke Burt, and we lay in the darkness holding hands, feeling the presence of Something bigger than ourselves hovering in the room. At that moment he voiced a prayer that launched our adventure of Christian parenting: "Lord, please heal Careen and give us this baby...but, Lord, if I'm not going to be the father that You know I need to be, then take this child back to heaven with You."

Until then our prayer life had been shallow. We mouthed a blessing before meals and attended church together, but being honest with God in front of each other was something new to us. We were both raised in Christian homes, but our own Christian walk together started that night. Two short years later, the Lord demonstrated His faithfulness to us again.

SCENE TWO: NOW YOU SEE HIM...

September 30, 1972
Dear Journal,

Today I watched a child disappear! I mean, seriously. I didn't know a kid could get lost so fast. He vanished while I watched him! Here's what happened:

I was in the cabin where we lived. (It was originally built as a gathering place for hunters and was situated in densely planted pine trees.) It has a screen porch across the front and I keep the outside door latched with a flip latch situated too high for a child to reach. While I was having a conversation with my mother-in-law, I watched two-year old Burt Jr, push a stool up to the door, climb on it, and flip the latch open. "What a smart little boy," I thought. I wasn't in a hurry to finish the conversation, certain that I knew where my child was going. He would be walking up the old timber road that ran in front of the cabin. We had walked that way many times.

When I hung up the phone I went outside to overtake him. After all, how fast can a two-year-old walk? Apparently pretty fast, because there was no sign of him! I walked for 30 minutes and couldn't find him. As much as I hated to admit it, the kid was gone! I didn't want to tell my mother-in-law, but I had to ask her to get in touch with Burt Sr., who was on a tractor somewhere. News travels fast when there's a distressed grandmother spreading the word. In 30 minutes our yard was full of people ready to make a search, some on horseback.

19

For four hours they combed the area around our cabin. Finally a close family friend, riding in his pickup truck, stopped at a house approximately a mile from our house. The people living there said they had noticed a little boy in a field behind their house. They said he had a dog with him and the animal wouldn't let them get close to him. When our friend began walking toward our child, our family dog must have recognized him because he let him pick up our son and bring him home. He was wet and his diaper had mud in it. He must have walked through a shallow pond. His reason for leaving was to go find the "twain." He apparently heard it because sure enough, he was going in the direction of the railroad tracks.

When Burt Sr. came home before Burt Jr. was found, he said, "Have you prayed about it?" I had, and I never felt any panic. It was no surprise to me to have our little boy returned unharmed and bemused by all the attention.

M eanwhile, about ten country miles away, my mother was enjoying one of her favorite pastimes — digging in her flower beds, pinching dead heads from blooming plants, and communing with the Lord in her spacious yard — when a disturbing feeling crept over her. Perplexed, she sat down in the half-rusted metal glider that occupied a quiet spot under the canopy of a monstrous, gnarled oak tree. There she prayed. Almost four hours passed before a sense of peace came over her, coinciding with the ringing of the telephone.

Burt Jr. and Bo: The Happy Wanderers

"Hey, Mom. I just called to tell you something that happened today. I was talking to Gran on the phone when I noticed Burt Jr. climbing up and opening the screen door to the porch…" I went on to tell her about my eventful day. She then told me her side of the story.

"I was outside working in the garden," she began, "when an overwhelming feeling came over me—a feeling that I needed to be praying. I didn't know who or what it was about, so I asked the Holy Spirit to lead me and pray through me. This went on for a long time, and then a sense of relief came over me. Just as I was getting up to go back to my gardening, you called and now you're telling me this."

I looked at our two-year-old, with his wet pants and sagging diaper, and let the impact of the miracle sink in—the peace I had felt, the urgent prayer alert Mom had gotten, and the release that came to her the exact moment her telephone rang. God's perfect timing was impossible to ignore.

So what did I learn from this? First, God's protection is available to us even when we don't know we need it. The Holy Spirit alerted someone to be our child's intercessor until he was safe—in this case, someone who loved him very much. Second, godly grandparents are a blessing. Since Burt Sr. and I are both products of parents and grandparents who relied on God, the charge became ours to pass this heritage on to our children.

Little did we know how much we would need God's help as our family multiplied. I was still trying to figure out how two people become one when we realized there would be three. Every time I adjusted to the new normal, my world shifted again…and again…and again…and again. If the birth of the first baby mimicked an earthquake of mammoth proportions, the addition of each subsequent child was like a series of aftershocks.

Even after the answers to prayer with our first son, the demands and needs of a growing family too often caused me to forget the miracles God consistently gave us. I could look at my beautiful healthy boys and wonder what was wrong with me. Why didn't I feel fulfilled the way I thought I should? I continued to complain to my journal.

August 27, 1979
Dear Journal,

This past month has been extremely difficult for me. I have a 3-month-old, along with a 2-year, 4-year, 7-year, and 9-year-old. I can't get everything done! I've cried almost every day over something. It bothers me because I don't seem to enjoy the children as I'd like to. I'm so tired I can't seem to cope. I tried aerobic dancing, hoping the exercise would make me feel better (and for the psychological effect of looking better), but it only added to my impossible list of responsibilities. I think my fatigue is a mixture of physical, mental, and spiritual. The mental pressure of trying to run the household (because Burt Sr. is too busy) and sensing the stresses of farming he's under is a big factor. I can't relax when he's working so hard because I feel guilty. I can't seem to convince myself taking care of children is enough work in itself. At the same time, I'm not content to stay in the children's world all the time. I feel so isolated when I do that.

Keeping a written account of the life my husband and I shared with five lively sons was like trying to describe the cars of a speeding train, but for me it became my means of survival. Those journals were my therapy when the guys were all young and I was struggling to keep it all together.

I yearned to be a competent mother. To me, this meant having children I could count on to listen and obey, not embarrass me in public — children who could see when I needed them to be on their best cooperative behavior. Often they failed to follow my script. I spent a few years trying to figure out a plan for my life, looking forward to the day my children weren't so needy. Then one day that all changed.

SCENE THREE: EPIPHANY

May 15, 1979
Dear Journal,

Today I was sitting in our house watching Clint and Josh playing with their little trucks on the floor. I guess I was vain enough to think that God had created me to do something really special, something that would make a difference to the world, and would be pleasing to Him. I sat dreaming about the possibilities that could be mine if I didn't have so many little ones to slow me down. I felt that my life was put on "hold" until my children didn't need me so much.

In the midst of all this thinking, I felt the Holy Spirit speak to my spirit. The question that came to me was, "If Jesus were here right now, where do you think He would be?" Then I knew the answer! He would be on the floor, playing with my sons. I thought about the verse, John 17:4 when Jesus says, "I glorified you on earth, having accomplished the work which you gave me to do."

What work has God given me to do? What does God want me to accomplish? For what purpose do I exist? I know the answer! To be the mother of five happy, well-adjusted, self-disciplined, Christian men!

A paradigm shift occurred at that moment. When I read the quote, "To the world you may be one person, but to one person you may be the world," I realized I was the world to five little persons. This insight changed everything.

People often asked me if I have a favorite son. I do. It's the one I'm talking to or looking at, at the moment. Trying to single out one of our boys over the others would be like taking a flower out of a perfect arrangement — it would diminish the effect. At the same time, there is nothing wrong with examining each different variety and appreciating its attributes and beauty. Individually, each son is fearfully and wonderfully made and has a magnificence of his own, but together they are God's arrangement, and I pray He is pleased.

From the moment God's voice spoke to my spirit, parenting our sons became my source of joy and fulfillment. I came to see them not as an interruption to my life but instead, the purpose of my life. Everything seemed to make more sense after that realization. Prioritizing was much easier. I learned to eliminate activities that weren't necessary or didn't contribute to the goal I now had before me, namely, to rear five godly men. I stopped waiting for them to grow up so I could make my mark in the world. I was satisfied that the process of parenting our sons was the thing that gave my life significance.

However, that doesn't mean I suddenly morphed into a placid mother hen who never got her feathers ruffled, who never lost patience with her children. I still had my meltdown moments. Read on.

October 19, 1980
Dear Journal,

Okay, I need to vent. It's a beautiful Saturday morning. I am seriously considering screaming. Clint and Josh are not getting along (the classic understatement). At least I realize they each want my attention. The phone rings: recipe for trouble. Clint tugs on the cord, refuses to dress himself, takes toys away from Josh. I put down the phone, spank Clint, who has on training pants. He crawls up on my bed and pulls the covers over his head. I finish the conversation, sitting beside him on the bed, patting his back. Just about the time he is comforted and satisfied with my affection, Josh comes in and lies down on top of Clint, making him yell. Then Clint swings a plastic bag of toys at Josh, hitting me instead. I abruptly hang up the phone and proceed to spank poor little Clint one more time. I give them the big sermon on sharing, send them into the living room to play with trucks, and I sit down at the kitchen table to reflect, When they start competing for the same toy, I get up with the threat of yet another spanking, and Josh says to Clint, "Hee-ah." Clint takes the offered truck and begins driving it peacefully. I feel satisfied that we're learning to share.

Thankfully, every day wasn't so bad, but I did feel life was passing me by, and all I did was change diapers and pick up things. Three times I had two children in diapers at the same time. During those years I found myself becoming aggravated at the older child, who would have been only two, for not being potty-trained. Then I felt guilty for letting my emotions get the best of me. I repeatedly berated myself for having to grit my teeth to get through the day. I looked calm and composed on the outside, but my emotions boiled inside. One day I let my feelings consume me, and in total frustration, I detonated them in my journal:

Nov. 13, 1980
Dear Journal,
*   When I got married, I'd never even said the "P" word! Now I'm surrounded by all sizes every day!*

I remember the feeling of being overwhelmed, overcome, and overworked. As the years went by, I became aware of certain things. For example, I realized that in moments of frustration I sometimes simply needed rest. Other times I needed time alone with my husband. More often than not, I needed spiritual refreshing.

Frequently my irritation was the result of not maintaining proper discipline with the boys. Eventually I learned how to manage them. I found out things get easier as children get older — if we lay the right foundation. My efforts became even more intentional when I realized we were forming our best friends for life. Finally, I came to terms with the fact that the children took time — *all* my time — and the only way I could manage my life was to say no to things that robbed me of my time with them. In her book, *How Do You Find the Time?* author Pat King (mother of eight) says, "If we have been called by God to be mothers, let's drop the activities that are making it so painful for us to enjoy our children…. We are adding a greater burden to society than we could ever compensate for with all our good deeds if we don't spend time training our children or if we don't spend time helping them to be secure as people."[1] I found that some of the activities I thought I needed to do could wait until our boys were older. There will always be social events, fundraisers, clubs, hobbies, volunteer opportunities, outside jobs, and innumerable worthy causes. Not that mothers should say no to everything, but the key is to know the commitments God is calling us to, and those that appease the expectations of other people.

For years, I fretted over what other mothers my age thought about my parenting. I wish I had gained the confidence then to know it didn't matter how someone else did it. As long as we obeyed the Lord and endeavored to raise our children for His honor, according to His principles, I didn't need to question my personal style, yet I compared my children's behavior and our routine — or lack of — to that of other people, and other mothers' styles to my own. I saw moms who had lives outside their homes, or whose children seemed happy being in daycare, and I wondered if I were missing it. I queried myself in my journal.

September 10, 1980
Dear Journal,

If spending time with my children is what I want to do, why does it matter what somebody else thinks? I'm devoted to my children, and if they are going to become spoiled because of it, I'll admit my mistake only after it is a proven fact.

That was a very good decision. I began to realize the more time I spent with them, the more I wanted to spend, and the more I enjoyed them. Several years later, I made the following observation.

May 14, 1985
Dear Journal,
    I realize something. Children are not a part of our life; they are *our life. When they become adults, we are rewarded the privilege of being a* part *of their lives.*

SCENE FOUR: NEW PECKING ORDER

July 10, 1979
Dear Journal,

I'd like for people to see us as a well-oiled machine, operating in perfect syncopation, all parts moving in rhythm with each other. It doesn't seem to happen that way (classic understatement). Sometimes I feel like we're a machine with all the parts flying in different directions and I'm trying to get them back in working order! I think I expend way too much energy trying to project an image to other people. I believe God has called us to be a witness for Him through our family, but that's not what I'm saying. I worry about how I look as a mother and how our boys perform for others. I want us to set a standard.

The desire to set a standard and prove to the world that I was an exemplary mother was tested when a sorority sister called to say she wanted to visit me. Never mind the fact I that I had five children under age ten, and she had never been married, plus she was a college dean. I was too caught up in anticipating a reunion with one of my bridesmaids whom I hadn't seen since my wedding to realize how challenging this would be. I wanted to appear efficient and impress her with my success as a fulltime mom. Here's the way I described the scene after she left.

July 25,1979
Dear Journal,

Today my good friend came for a visit. When she got here at 5:00 p.m. I was finally vacuuming the living room. I had sent the older two boys to take an early bath so they wouldn't harass the younger ones later when I bathed them. I hoped it looked like a routine at the end of a typical day, but it was such a masquerade. I had tossed a Christmas ornament that doubled as a toy into a cabinet just a moment before she entered the door. Earlier today I threatened the boys within an inch of their lives if they didn't get their mess off the floor. Of course all summer the mess had been accumulating — construction projects made from Legos, collections of bugs and rocks, summer reading books, random tennis shoes, assorted cars and trucks. I hoped to look confident and composed, but inside I wanted to hide in a cave!

Once my friend arrived, the boys were incorrigible! Each one was determined to be the center of attention. I was embarrassed because I thought I looked like an incompetent mother.

Having someone different in the house always caused commotion. It didn't matter who the person was. Everyone who entered the door was the boys' potential audience, and each of them wanted to be the star of the show. The way they went about achieving that depended on their personality. Typically Burt Jr. got the most attention since he was the oldest and the most visible, and Josh got noticed because he was the youngest. The others had to see what they could do not to be overlooked. They also didn't want to be ignored by me, and when they realized whoever was there had my attention, it caused intense competition. My friend made an observation I had been too close to the scene to recognize.

"With the addition of each new family member," she said, "a shift of position in the family has to be made, a new pecking order established. The only position that doesn't change is the first-born, but everybody else feels threatened by the new kid on the block." Being an only child had sheltered me from that experience. Her remark gave me good insight; it was probably the first time I looked at the world through my children's eyes. Until then, I only thought about how their behavior affected me.

Maybe I became a better mother that day. At least it made me stop and analyze their behavior instead of trying to control them to suit my moods. That didn't mean I didn't discipline them, or at least make the effort to, but I could better understand what their actions were trying to communicate. I became more conscious of trying to make each one feel appreciated and singled out, but at the same time not let them be obnoxious, and that was a tight wire to walk. It took every bit of my mental and physical energy to maintain that balance.

I also had needs of my own. For instance, I functioned better when there was order around me and with five boys, ages nine, seven, three, one, and newborn, order didn't always happen. Our situation was compounded by a farming schedule that was demanding and exhausting. Burt Sr. wanted our farm to look as successful and impressive as I wanted the family to look. For a season, we had difficulty agreeing on priorities.

August 26, 1979
Dear Journal,

It's 2:45 a.m. I can't sleep. This is a rare thing for me! Thoughts keep boiling in my head and I can't seem to turn them off. I'm out of harmony with Burt, and probably with the Lord too, and I don't like it. I feel like the whole summer has gone by and I haven't even seen my husband. We have hardly had time to talk to each other. Everywhere I look, something is a mess. The yards are the worst. I think that's what bothering me so bad, because I can't get this done by myself and Burt hasn't got time to think about it.

I think he should care because I care. It's making me sick, and I simply must get my head together about it. The windows are dirty and the basement is awful, all piled up. I need to have things clean and neat. I wish Burt could understand how important that is to me. Meanwhile, he's making sure there are perfectly clean furrows between the rows of peanuts, or cotton, or whatever.

Tomorrow school starts. I'm sad about that too. I guess I don't want to see the summer end. The boys aren't ready to get back into the school routine either; that really makes it hard.

I want to get everything organized, windows washed, carpet cleaned, desk and office neat. I wish Burt wouldn't work so hard and have such long hours. It's not that he's selfish. He hasn't played golf or tennis, except when he played with the children on our beach vacation. I wish I could release him from the expectations I put on him. I want him to be available for the boys, attentive to my needs, helpful with projects around the house, yet provide for our family. I also need his physical closeness, but I feel so pulled apart and depleted by the needs of the children, whom I love with all my heart.

Obviously, there was some turmoil going on about this time, both in me as well as in the children. It was destined to surface eventually. Consumed with responsibilities of work and parenting, we must have missed some signs, because a few weeks after my friend's visit we had an incident that almost devastated me. This incident isn't easy to write about, and it represents the lowest point of my motherhood experience. It served a good purpose, however, because it caused us to realize how critical Burt Sr.'s involvement was in our sons' development. They needed their daddy.

SCENE FIVE: NEEDING DADDY

September 3, 1979
Dear Journal,

   Today I'm writing about a painful event that took place this past
week. Wednesday afternoon Gran came over with two of her friends
for a visit. They wanted to see the new baby. It was just about the
time the boys were getting off the bus from school. They came in, hot
and thirsty, and all the ladies started asking them questions about
their day. Burt Jr. was tired and resentful, and acted very rudely. Of
course this embarrassed me because I wanted to look good for Gran
and her friends. After they left, I reprimanded him (I was mad), and
I told him he had to write, "I will be polite to guests" 100 times. He
became indescribably upset, accused me of not loving him, and said
he was going to jump out the window. He said that I had fussed at
him all summer (he was right), and that I didn't care if he died or
not. I felt I was looking into the eyes of a stranger.

   I left his room completely devastated. I was so shocked I didn't
know what to say. I cried and cried out of desperation; Adam and
Jed tried to comfort me. I went back to Burt Jr.'s room a little later
and found that he had removed the screen and was standing on the
ledge of his second-story window looking at the concrete below. He
could easily have fallen. I had never felt like such a failure. I was at
such a complete loss as to what to do that I just backed away from
the scene, stunned.

   That night Burt Sr. and I talked everything out. We discussed
everything from Burt Jr.'s needs, to my frustration over the yard, the
unfinished things in the house, and Burt Sr.'s busyness. I laid the

responsibility for Burt Jr. at Burt Sr.'s feet, and I was right about that. I told him he was overworked and that he was neglecting his responsibilities as priest of our home. The Holy Spirit took over then, and showed him that he needed to make more time to be with the children, as well as be the disciplinarian God expected him to be.

The very next morning another incident happened. Burt Jr. did something as he and Adam were getting ready for school that deserved a spanking. Burt Sr. spanked him, but it only produced resentment. Knowing he couldn't leave him in that state, he spanked him again, and this time Burt Jr. showed real repentance. His daddy stayed with him in his room and counseled and comforted him until everything was settled. I didn't feel that we had gotten to the root of the attitude, but I sensed we were on our way.

From that episode, my husband and I knew changes had to be made. I felt I had been trying to parent alone. The night of Burt Jr.'s meltdown, Burt Sr. and I had a serious talk. We agreed he needed to be more intentional about spending time with each of our sons. As he did, our home life started to change. Burt started taking Burt Jr. with him frequently, and we both saw the fruit of that endeavor. One day as they were at their grandfather's pond walking and looking for arrowheads, Burt Jr. stopped, looked at his father, and said, "Dad, I just enjoy walking with you."

The Lord empowered Burt Sr. to become a wonderful dad. I learned to appreciate the moments he shared with our sons. He was a companion to the boys, and I enjoyed watching them interact with each other. When they were young (probably around four), he took them with him whenever he could. They rode in his truck, the tractor, the fishing boat—whatever he offered. They anticipated the moment he would arrive home to wrestle with them on the floor and chase them around the house, a game they never tired of. The only problem was, because he kept long farmer's hours, especially in the summer, it was often late when the house became quiet for the night. He also typically wasn't home when I needed the most help: the late afternoon around 5:00 p.m. (the cook-dinner-take-baths-put-away-toys-brush-teeth-prepare-for-bed time of day) when everybody was tired and whiny, including me. My problem was not the fact I couldn't do what needed doing; it was just that I craved time for myself. By the time everybody settled down for the night, I was slammed.

Recovery time for me turned out to be Saturday mornings. When the boys were young, before they got involved with hunting activities, traveling baseball teams, sleepovers, campouts, etc., I savored Saturday mornings.

SCENE SIX: SATURDAY SABBATH

May 10, 1980
Dear Journal,

It's a Saturday morning. Burt and Adam are old enough to take care of themselves. That means they can get their own cereal (Cheerios or Life, maybe even sugared Fruit Loops by this time). Jed is at the age that he wants to be wherever those two are.

Saturday mornings are MY TIME. This is the only day that I get to laze around in the bedroom, loving every minute that I can prop myself on some pillows and write in my journal. This is a moment of catharsis for me, writing down the events of the week, expressing my frustrations as well as my blessings. I love it when the older ones get their own breakfast, bringing their bowls to the sink after they finish, and go outside to play. I love for Clint and Josh to wake up late, come to my room where we cuddle up together and they watch cartoons.

Unfortunately, that rarely happens.

What really goes on is this: Burt and Adam get their cereal. They come into my bedroom with their bowls brimming (and sloshing) with milk and set up camp on the floor to watch cartoons, usually the classic ones like "Bugs Bunny" or "Roadrunner." This morning Clint piled on top of me at 7:30 a.m., diaper smelling. (He fell asleep at 5:00 p.m. yesterday on the living room couch and I left him there all night, so he is well rested.) Being of the submissive disposition *that he is, he waits until I get up, and then follows me to the bathroom, begging for his cereal. As I am getting his bowl, I turn to find Joshua coming into the kitchen dragging his blanket. I fix him a bottle, put him in his bed, and lie back down. In a few minutes Jed gets up, disturbing Joshua. I call for Clint, who is eating his cereal, to go and get Josh out of bed. He does, and proceeds to take away his blanket. Josh yells. I wait a few minutes and then I hear Clint wail. I go into the kitchen to find Josh sitting on top of the table in Clint's bowl of cereal. I clean up the mess, put Josh in the utility room sink. While I am on the telephone (about 8:15a.m.), Josh finds my billfold (including checks, money, pictures, etc.) and submerges it in his bath water. I dry everything, dress Josh and Clint, feed Josh cereal, and send them out to play. Shortly afterwards, Josh comes in, covered in mud. I clean him up, putting him down for a morning nap. It's now about 10:45a.m. I'm ready to go back to bed!*

Need I say more?

It's important for a mother to find her place of solace. Mine happened to be writing in journals, particularly on Saturday mornings. In those times I expressed my annoyances, recorded prayers, connected with my Creator, and restored my balance. Putting thoughts and impressions on paper helped me examine a situation. It helped me deposit my feelings so I didn't have to carry them, thus freeing my mind for the next set of challenges. The fact is if I had not written things down as they happened, I wouldn't remember those times of exasperation. The scenes of life move in such rapid succession, our memories become a mélange of sights, sounds, and smells, and the episodes seem to collide with one another.

Memories of motherhood scenes resurface unexpectedly, such as when I found a petrified raisin in a child's old lunchbox, or firecrackers in a coat pocket, or felt dents on a metal bat (the result of using rocks for batting practice). From time to time I came across an article of clothing left from a particular season, such as a Little League baseball uniform with red clay stains, or a pair of ripped jeans from the day the five-year-old fell and broke his arm. Reading my journals helped me recall the emotions I experienced when that event happened. At the time I wasn't always thinking about the future; I was simply trying to survive the moment. Sometimes I see how a seemingly insignificant episode became an important piece of the family puzzle, and it helps me understand the people my children have become.

The motherhood stage is difficult. It's insistent, demanding, both physically and emotionally draining. At times I felt I had handed out all the bread I had, and it wasn't enough to satisfy the ones I had to feed. I needed desperately to go back to the Master for a fresh supply. God is the only one who can fully refresh us and supply what we need, but the way we seek Him is unique to our individual personalities. The important thing is to know there is only one Source that satisfies all our needs and to learn how to draw from that Source.

During the first three years of childrearing I had a fairly consistent routine of quiet time with the Lord during the boys' afternoon nap. As I played a favorite song on the stereo after they calmed down, I sensed an aura of peace settling around me. It was a time of the day I looked forward to and it provided restoration for my soul, as it says in Psalm 23, "He restores my soul." If anybody needs a refreshing of the soul, it's a busy mother.

Sometimes Burt Sr. was able to come home for a break in his day, and it was satisfying to know this time offered a respite for him as well. Besides the personal benefit of restoring our souls, our homes need to be a refuge from the world for our family. As hectic as a mom's routine is, our husbands and children have their own set of challenges. If the home doesn't become the place of restoration and comfort they need, where else will they go?

I wish I could say I followed the perfect plan for soul restoration over the next several years, but as the babies kept coming, it became increasingly difficult to stay with the schedule. I had to deal with the guilt of that at least once a day. My advice for young women is to store up as much of the God's Word as possible before children come. Of course we continue to need this time every day, but the demands of an active family coupled with fatigue make it harder to maintain the habit. Sometimes a Scripture or another inspirational thought will come to the forefront and sustain us in moments of exhaustion and turmoil. Listen to calming music in the background of our busyness can help sooth nerves and tempers as well.

It's also beneficial to bond with other Christian mothers who not only appreciate the importance of spending time with the Source of strength, but who can understand and pray for us when we are overwhelmed. As our boys got older, it was easier to connect with other women in fellowship groups. To know others who were raising their children with the same values we had encouraged me.

One of my favorite books is *A Place of Quiet Rest* by Nancy Leigh DeMoss. Her words never cease to convict me: "Developing intimacy with the Lord Jesus requires a conscious, deliberate choice. It is a choice to spend time sitting at His feet and listening to His word, even when there are other good things that demand our attention....Not until we make pursuing Him our highest priority and goal in life will we begin to fulfill the purpose for which He created us."[2] The main thing is to stop our constant activity and fretting about all the jobs that need doing and spend quality time in the Lord's presence. I don't want to make it sound easy because it's not. There were occasions when I thought the only opportunity I had to rest was in the dentist chair!

SCENE SEVEN: PERFECT SEVEN

July 1,1981

Dear Journal,

Well, it's done. We're not having any more children. We made our decision and followed through almost like a dream. It was the hardest decision I've ever had to make. I guess I was afraid of losing something that has held us close. I felt like part of my body had died, but something more emotional than physical. Burt kept reassuring me that it was the right thing to do. He assured me that our feelings of closeness we would never lose. He said that we would have another ministry or combined effort of some sort that would unite us that would probably be even more fulfilling. That gave me a great sense of relief. I don't have any idea what it might be, of course. We talked about the possibility of having some kind of ministry for other families. I would love to see us function together as a unit and have our boys minister along with us. I know there is such a concerted evil effort to destroy families, and only the Holy Spirit can fight it. I believe the day will come that people will be around us and will have a feeling of love for their children and children for their parents just from being in our presence. Is that what the Scripture in Malachi 4:5-6 means when it says, "Behold I will send you Elijah the prophet...and he shall turn the hearts of the fathers to their children and the hearts of the children to the fathers"? Has He given us the "spirit of Elijah"?

This idea excites me! If this, or something like it, is what God is going to do with us, then I am excited and can't wait to get started! However, I know without a shadow of a doubt, that right now is the time to lay the foundation for the task we have before us. I know that we must make God's perfect will operate in our own family before we will be able to effectively minister to anyone else.

Perfect Seven

Once this decision was consummated, I was ready to enter into a new phase of life. I began to see the older boys having moments of independence, and the prospect of life without diapers was looking better all the time. There was a new sense of freedom without the threat of pregnancy always in the wings. Now I could look forward to some semblance of a routine, more time for relaxation for me, and the possibility of having a house without plastic baby paraphernalia.

However, it seemed every time I thought we were ready for our debut, I discovered we needed a few more dress rehearsals! My desire to present the all-together model family was usually juxtaposed with a scene such as this one:

July 14, 1982
Dear Journal,
Tonight was frustrating! At 6:45 p.m. I was dashing through the house, snatching random toys, straightening sofa pillows, and

getting dinner ready before a group of young married couples was scheduled to arrive at 7:30. None of the couples have children yet, and we are supposed to be preparing them for parenting! At 7:15 Burt came home from the field with the boys. I had made the decision it would be easier for me if they went with him than to stay in the house. Bad call.

Our guests got here before the guys returned – of course! They came back sweaty, dirty, and hungry. Josh had a pocket filled with seeds and trash, which he dumped on the kitchen floor I had just swept. I told him to hold the dustpan while one of our guests swept up his mess. He was obstinate, so Burt Jr. assumed the parent role and used some physical coercion to make him cooperate. This infuriated Josh, who doesn't like being manhandled by a big brother, so blows were exchanged, followed by wails and words. By then some of the wails and words were coming from me, because I knew other people were observing this fiasco! Daddy, meanwhile, had gone to take a shower and clean up. I guess he figured keeping the boys out of my hair for a while completed his job.

Everybody was huddled in the kitchen. (Why do people automatically congregate in the kitchen?) I hid behind my hospitality mask, served Sloppy Joes to the boys, hissed threats to them under my breath, and ushered the visitors into the living room, leaving the children eating their meal. Before long blood sugar levels rose, tempers calmed, and amiability reigned over the dinner scene. Then I wished our guests had come into the kitchen to see that our children can actually behave with some decorum!

Our house has always been a gathering spot. Some days, in the midst of the chaos, I wanted to run away to a hotel and hide, and sometimes Burt Sr. and I did. Having willing grandparents and trustworthy teenage sitters made this possible. Jesus himself took His disciples with Him to get away from the crowd, and He got up before anyone else to pray (see Mark 1:35). As the demands of our family increased, I understood this need more every day.

The gift of hospitality is a grace I believe God gave us to be a witness for Him. We didn't try to entertain, but simply shared our family with anyone who wanted to come over. This opened doors for us and gave us a community of people who blessed us as we hoped we blessed them. Although the boys are no longer living at home, our house still has a revolving door. Burt Sr. and I both espouse authenticity, and the presence of outsiders who observe how we do life keeps us accountable, as well as vulnerable. We have to depend on the Holy Spirit to keep us in line so we won't fail to be a good example of what a Spirit-led family is supposed to look like.

SCENE EIGHT:
MESSING AROUND

July 23, 1982
Dear Journal

    Burt Jr., Adam, and their dad came home from combining wheat the other night with three rabbits. It was hard to say which of the three of them was more delighted with their catch. They put the rabbits in buckets on the screen porch and fed them carrots and other delicacies. The rabbits jumped out every night, creating an uncontrollable pleasure for Joshua (age 3), and an annoyance for me. Finally, upon realizing that the porch smelled like a city zoo, I told them the rabbits had to go. Dad told them they had to release the rabbits in the field where they found them so they could find food. Since we were leaving for the beach the next day, I told Burt Jr. and Adam to clean the porch. They cooperated that afternoon. Burt Jr. vacuumed thoroughly and Adam mopped the floor with Lysol. The only problem was that the rabbits were now loose on the porch. Eventually the boys went to bed, and I expected Burt to take the rabbits and set them free when he left for the field to check the irrigation system. When he didn't, I got very upset. I felt that the family didn't respect my wishes to have a neat, clean place to live, and I was hurt and angry at their insensitivity. I was trying to get organized for our upcoming beach trip and I needed some cooperation! I felt very hurt and unappreciated. It made me have some weird thoughts, like maybe I wanted girls instead of dirty boys!

Finally Burt came back and announced that he was going to catch the rabbits. I don't know if he sensed my acrimony or not, but I think he realized he had made a good call!

Rabbits and a Friend

S tudying the basic temperament types helped me understand myself and how I parented our children. One aspect of my temperament is the negative effect chaos and clutter has on me. This posed a big problem because it seemed chaos and clutter characterized every activity, especially when the boys were out of school for the summer.

In spite of my complaints, I believe growing up on a farm in the country was the best thing that could have happened to our family of boys. They never begged to live in town, and it was usually their friends coming to our house rather than the other way around. The messes typically resulted because they and their friends were doing something they absolutely loved. One of their most enjoyable activities was the one I just described — chasing and catching rabbits in the wheat fields.

They also loved seizing and bringing home anything that moved. Over the years, we have had as house guests the following: frogs, lizards, rabbits, turtles, dogs, cats, a baby fox, a very angry raccoon, a wounded hawk, rats (which provided food for the hawk), two baby deer, coyote pups, and seventeen baby turkeys. Some of these visitors didn't stay very long! And did I mention the snakes? I felt like I operated a Home for Boys, a Bed and Breakfast, and an Animal Sanctuary all rolled into one!

There were times I didn't think Burt Sr. had a clue about what was important to me, or worse, that he did know and wouldn't do anything about it. Sometimes I believed I was fighting a battle alone. On occasions when we pulled together as a married couple, and I felt his support, it was wonderful, but for a few years it seemed a lonely road, and I

Josh and a Pet (Not)

would feel sorry for myself. My frustrations generally related to my physical surroundings, or to the fact that Burt Sr. didn't always do things according to my timetable. It was hard for me to function smoothly when things got out of place and I felt disregarded. Take this episode for instance.

September 24, 1982
Dear Journal,
    Sorry. I just need to vent! I am so irritated!

Two months ago we had a fish fry at a friend's house. We took our bug light because they needed an extra one. When it was time to leave, Burt didn't get it because we were all tired and ready to go. Said he'd get it later. I knew he was tired, but heck, I had to round up all the children and their paraphernalia and get them in the car. It wasn't that the bug light was all that important; it's just that I didn't want to have to remember to go back for it. It annoyed me then and I've let it marinade in my mind all this time, and now I am exasperated!

This afternoon's episode sent me over the top. The boys came home from quail hunting with a bag of dead birds — and a not-so-dead one that came back to life! This last-mentioned thing got loose in our living room! The boys thought it was riotous! I thought so too, but not in the same way. The situation was exacerbated by the fact that, along with the boys, Burt Sr. thought it was comical. The bird hunkered down under the wood in the fireplace! I got mad because Burt didn't get him out immediately, and I told him so. Then I felt better.

What all this boils down to is this: little irritations add up to become a great big pile of rubble. My not saying anything about the bug light had festered in my spirit for two months, and then I let a situation I'll probably look back and laugh at years from now, get to me. What I'm seeing is, because I'm so busy with the children, I stuff feelings down inside without discussing them, and resentments build. Eventually they come to the surface, usually all blown out of proportion. Maybe that's why couples divorce after years of marriage. Once the family is gone and their minds are not otherwise occupied, the annoyances that were never dealt with emerge. I pray that never happens to us.

Thank God Burt Sr. came to understand my needs as the years went by. Also, now that our sons have homes and families of their own, they appreciate what it takes to maintain order. I can read this journal entry now and see the humor in it. A wild bird alive in the house would be funny — if it happened in somebody else's living room!

If I were writing a script about our family's life, it would probably turn into a comedy. Learning to laugh is a vital trait, and research proves negativity is a drain of both emotional and physical energy. Because laughter refreshes us emotionally and physically, Moms need to find a source of humor—even if it's reading funny cards in the grocery store—and nothing amuses me as much as the interaction and verbal exchanges among our family members. When we reminisce, it's invariably about some of the times at which I was the most exasperated, and now even I think they're funny.

Any time we laugh about family memories, the beach vacation from you-know-where usually comes up. Funny thing...I love reliving this particular occasion. The chaos, the fatigue, the irritations—they all blend together to form a mosaic of happy family memories. At the time I wrote this, however, I wasn't thinking about the good stories that would come from it. My cork was about ready to pop.

SCENE NINE: STRANGE FAMILY VACATION

July 19, 1981
Dear Journal,

Well, the day has finally come. It's Friday night before Sunday, when we will leave for two weeks to St. George Island. I've never had to pack a Port-a-Crib for a trip, take all our groceries, manage two children in diapers away from home, or be gone for that long on a vacation.

I face the coming weeks with mixed emotions. I envision relaxed evenings, late afternoon strolls on the beach, time with Burt... I wonder how it will be. If my preparation time last night is any indication, it will be a disaster! Here's my night:

Burt had to go to a meeting tonight and I was making a quick sandwich for him. While I was in the kitchen doing this, Joshua was downstairs in the basement. Also downstairs were things to take to the beach, including all the groceries, since there are no grocery stores on St. George Island. Burt Jr. came into the kitchen and made this announcement: "Mom, Josh is downstairs playing in the groceries."

Dropping my knife in the sink, I went to investigate. I found Joshua downstairs, sitting in a pile of loose tea, holding an empty tea bag box. He had opened every one of the family size bags and scattered the tea everywhere. I didn't scream or cry, as I wanted to do; I calmly asked Burt Jr. if he would get the vacuum and clean it up. He must have sensed my desperation because he willingly complied.

Putting his arm around me, he said, "Mom, you know I wouldn't do this for anybody else but you." It's times like these that I feel so guilty about fussing at him. Maybe I'll have time to think about that while we're at the beach.

I marched Josh upstairs and plopped him in the bed. No hugs. No kiss. No prayers. I left him crying.

I had packed mine and Burt's clothes that afternoon while Josh was napping, leaving our suitcases open on our bed. Apparently Josh had discovered them, because when I came back to our room, I found all the neatly folded clothes in a heap on the floor! Well, I absolutely lost it! I went back to Joshua's room, snatched him from his bed, and spanked his legs with the first thing I could get my hands on — a plastic hairbrush — because I couldn't find my paddle. I made him pick up every piece of clothing and then ordered him back to bed. He went, crying of course, and I felt so ashamed of myself and utterly frustrated. Maybe when we get to St. George I can figure out what to do with him.

The next morning, as we were loading the car to leave, Joshua tossed a cantaloupe down the basement steps. Seeds, pulp, and juice spattered the wall and the steps. I didn't get upset over this because Burt Sr. was here to help me. He took charge — as only a dad can. While we cleaned the mess and finished packing the car, Josh sat calmly in his car seat and gave us no more trouble all the way to the beach.

The boys complained because we got off so late. I was as perturbed as they were. Why couldn't we just get the family neatly organized and off on a road trip on time? Other people seemed to do it. Why couldn't we?

My farmer husband didn't last the full two weeks as planned. I wasn't surprised. We had friends there with us, along with their college-age niece, so he decided to ride home with them, and the niece would stay and ride back with me. He would go back to check on the farm, and the boys and I could enjoy the beach a few days longer. He also knew I had support from my parents who were staying in a house next door, in addition to help from our new college friend. It appeared to be a perfect plan.

The truth was, I had never felt such a sinking feeling as I did when I saw the children's father jump in the car with our friends and drive away. I felt like Atlas holding up the world. The thought of having the responsibility of all the boys, keeping our college-age guest amused and not bored with us, and having to clean the beach house and pack everything up by myself was more than overwhelming. I wanted to appear stress-free for my parents' sake, as well as prove to our guest how well I could manage my children. The boys, however, were delighted. They had a new audience and naturally, each of them was competing for her attention in his own way. It was the first time they'd had a pretty college girl to play with!

The next four days went acceptably well until we had to pack up to go home. I spent most of the morning crying. Burt Jr. prayed for me, although I'm sure at his age, he couldn't imagine what was wrong. He and Adam did the best that nine and eleven year old boys could do, and we finally pulled away from the beach house at 3:00 p.m. Checkout time was at 12 noon.

Josh had been such a model passenger on the way down to the beach, sitting in his car seat and not creating any kind of disturbance. (After the cantaloupe episode he must have thought he'd better do something to get back in our good graces.) I naturally wasn't expecting any different behavior on the way back. I was driving our car with the grandparents following me in their car. They took Adam, Jed, and Clint with them, leaving me with Burt Jr., Josh, and our new friend. It didn't take me long to realize that Josh was not content to stay in the back seat with a beautiful passenger riding in the front, especially when she kept turning around to play with him. The seat belt/child-restraint law was not as stringent as it is now, so Josh crawled over the seat where he had all her attention as well as the contents of her purse to play with, including her make-up. I sensed I had lost the battle.

On the trip back, my dad dozed off at the wheel and ran onto the shoulder of the road. I think it might have been at that point I saw my parents at a new phase in life: tired from all the baby-sitting help they'd given me. I guess I had taken their health and energy for granted until then, and this was a hint for me to be more attentive to them.

Anyway, we made it home safely, only to find that the downstairs freezer door had been left ajar while we were gone and the contents were thawed.

So while I cooked the thawed food, trying to save what I could, our newly acquired "nanny" entertained the boys. At this point I didn't care what the children did, as long as they stayed out of my way. The young lady provided a wonderful distraction.

She and the boys concocted more amusements than I thought possible, like "candle wars" in the upstairs bedrooms. This meant they went into the attic, found Christmas candles that were soft from the summer heat and threw them at the target, which was one of them. Whenever someone missed the intended victim, the wax would hit the wall, leaving an oily spot.

This no doubt begs the question, why did I let all this go on? The answer is, after I discovered what they were doing, the damage was already done; they were having such a good time in the process; I was able to get some of my work done without interference; the resident babysitter didn't seem to mind. Whatever got broken or dirty in the process could be repaired. Somehow at this point, it seemed easier to repair the damage than try to prevent it. (Those who have children will surely understand what I've just written.)

After our vacation experience, I saw that I had learned some things about myself, such as how comparing my schedule with that of friends made me feel like a failure. Again, I became introspective regarding my style of parenting.

August 24, 1981
Dear Journal,

When I watch another mother who is organized and scheduled, it makes me almost resentful. Why can she do it and I can't? I'm wondering whether it's really worth it. I don't know if I prefer my less structured approach or if I'm just jealous. I want to shift the blame to my husband. I rationalize that it's because of his unpredictable schedule that we are like we are. He doesn't care if we have breakfast early or later when he can come back to the house after getting his morning started, and I never know what time he'll be in for the night meal. But bedtime is absolutely hopeless! Even on the nights that I have them clean and ready for bed, Burt invariably takes them out on the farm with him, either to check the irrigation system or to look for a rabbit. Of course the boys love it! Some nights it's 11:30 before I get everybody settled!

Here's another factor: I'm not sure if my concern over our loose schedule is because I really need a schedule, or if my concern is over what other people seem to think of our lifestyle. If I knew that, then I might know what to do about it. Also, I don't really know how the children are happiest, with a schedule or without.

About a month later, I had a chance to evaluate my thinking. Some things were beginning to become clear to me.

September 19, 1981
Dear Journal,

We have been back from St. George about a month. After reading some of the thoughts from our vacation, I see that things are much better now. For some reason, being with the children every minute made me appreciate and enjoy them more, rather than get tired of them. Our new college friend spent eight days with us after we got home. The children performed for her the whole time she was here. She played with them so hard I couldn't do anything to stop them. Finally I conceded that I'd let them have fun and give up trying to keep them quiet.

In August, she and I took the older two, plus three friends, to Columbus to celebrate Adam's ninth birthday. As we were walking in the mall, I ran into a former student. This student asked her how she dealt with the chaos at the Strange house. She replied, yes it was noisy indeed, but she had never seen a happier bunch of children. That made me feel so good!

The way I feel right now, I don't really care what anybody says about the way we raise our children. If we let them be noisy and free, so what? As long as they enjoy being at home and being with us, I don't care how noisy they are. The proof to me is how devoted the boys are to the Lord and to each other and to us. Being away with them at the beach has made me realize that nothing in the world is more important than being with them. I used to think that my ministry was to my friends and to people in need, and the children got the leftover time. Now my priorities are totally reversed. If my children can't be a part of my ministry to somebody else, then the "somebody else" will have to find somebody else to minister to them!

By the end of that summer I felt satisfied about getting to know our children better. With that attitude, we delved into the school routine. I had the feeling I had settled into a comfortable seat to enjoy a performance, but when the curtain rose, I was stunned. Without warning, we had pre-adolescent children. Our family gyrated into a rapid succession of scene changes, while I became the frantic director trying to choreograph the characters and make them stick to a script.

Once school started, I had a bit more free time, but different demands. Now I had to conform to their schedules. And to friends' schedules. And extracurricular activities. My life seemed to be steadily gaining momentum, including moments when I felt completely out of control.

ACT II

THE BOYHOOD STAGE

For I, too, was once my father's son, tenderly
loved by my mother as an only child.
Proverbs 4:3 (NLT)

SCENE ONE: SCHOOL DAYS BEGIN

August 28, 1981
Dear Journal,

School started last Monday. Jed is in kindergarten, Adam is in the fourth grade and Burt is in the sixth. I wanted to take them to school every morning just because I yearned to be with them and start their day. Finally I decided to put them on the bus, with the promise that I would pick them up whenever possible. Burt Jr. kept insisting that he didn't want the responsibility of looking after Jed on the bus. I think that's because he's afraid Jed might get teased and cry. I took them to school Monday and Tuesday, but Wednesday they met the bus. Burt Jr. offered to let Jed sit with him, which made Jed grab him around the waist and hug him. Adam was so sweet; he offered to walk Jed to his classroom. So they left for school happy.

On the first day of school, Burt Sr. went with me. It was so much easier with him along. I saw other mothers with tears in their eyes, and it made me feel better to know other moms also found this hard. Although I do enjoy the lack of chaos when some of the children are gone, I still like the feeling of being close to them. I'm glad I can enjoy a quiet house for a while. I guess if I didn't, it would be too hard to let the boys leave. Sometimes I wonder how I will handle it when they all leave for good, but then I realize that our house will probably always be full of activity and guests. I'll bet we'll never have a dull house!

When Burt Sr. and I returned from taking them to school on Monday, I found Clint and Josh in our bedroom watching "Captain

Kangaroo." *(Emma came early to stay with them while we were gone.) When I saw them, I thought how cute they were, and I was so thankful we didn't stop with three!*

I've made a huge discovery regarding scheduling. With school in session, schedule is everything! *I realize also that it is up to me to see that the schedule is carried out. I have to plan my activities so I won't be too tired to enforce the routine. That takes some discipline on my part. It means leaving off too many outside activities, cutting out chatty phone conversations. The wonderful thing is, when I let these kinds of things go, I am free to enjoy the children. I'm not as irritable because I'm not as pressured to get so much done. I'm content in knowing that I'm better organized with their lunches, their clothes — everything. I'm also released from the struggle of trying to be something to other people. Right now I'd rather be everything to them.*

Growing Boys

To this day, I don't know how women work fulltime and foster a successful family. I know it can be done, because I have friends who did it. However, taking care of our clan was all I could handle, even with the help from grandparents and other lifesavers. Only God knows exactly what each individual needs, and I realized I had to tap into His wisdom to know how to manage my cast of characters. This took all my time. Often I found an answer in some of my readings, but at times I obeyed the impulse I felt inside, which I came to recognize was God's Spirit giving me insight and wisdom.

A few years later, when all the boys were in school, I went back into high school teaching. This was all part of His great plan and His perfect timing—but I'll get to that later in the story. Meanwhile, I continued to make adjustments for the changing needs and emotions of three boys in school and two at home with me.

SCENE TWO: BOYS MATURE (OR NOT)

September 21, 1981
Dear Journal,

What a day! I have really had a lot of pieces of the puzzle begin to fit today. It all began this morning (as days usually do) when Burt Jr. wanted to stay home from school because of a sore throat. I went upstairs to work at my desk, leaving him downstairs with Emma, helping to entertain Clint and Josh. I heard sounds of the dumb-waiter sliding up and down. In a few minutes, I heard Josh wailing. I didn't associate the two sounds, but shortly afterwards Burt Jr. yelled, "Mom, Josh mashed his finger in the dumbwaiter." "Tell Emma to come get me if she needs me," I replied. In a few minutes she came up carrying the baby, still crying, his little hand swollen and red. Then I found out the truth.

Burt Jr. had put Josh in the dumbwaiter to "give him a ride." I was so stunned I couldn't process the thought! It was incredulous to think that a "mature" 11-year-old would put a 2-year-old in a wooden box enclosed in a small elevator shaft (a.k.a. the dumbwaiter) and send him on a ride! I was so focused on what to do with him that I almost ignored Josh's hand, which was swelling more by the minute.

I called Burt Sr. on the farm radio, asking him to come home, but not to be too hard on Burt Jr. – although I was exasperated with him. He found him in his room. We acknowledged the need for wisdom. Burt talked to Burt Jr., they came out of his room together, and we all prayed for Josh's hand. We also told Burt Jr. he had to go with us to the doctor's office. All the way there he repeatedly said how sorry he was. Thankfully Josh's little hand was okay, nothing broken.

My feelings were ambivalent toward Burt Jr. I expected more maturity from him, and I didn't know how to handle him.

Then tonight, something else happened. He and Adam were showering in our bathroom, and they got into my make-up and good perfume. I was totally put out with them, and grabbed the paddle, ready for revenge. Burt Jr. got extremely upset. Apparently Adam was the instigator, and punishment at this point would not have exposed what I realized was a deeper-rooted issue. I sensed some things lay beneath the surface. After some discussion, I agreed to let them tell me what they wanted from me. The list was surprising:

1. *Mom to always go to church with them (not stay home to rest).*
2. *Something to look forward to on weekends, i.e. having a friend over, or shopping with me, or an occasional ballgame or movie.*
3. *Story time or Bible reading with me every night, with or without Daddy (because he didn't "snuggle" the way I did).*
4. *Time with me in the afternoons to help them study.*

All this seems to add up to two conclusions:

1. *They want me involved in their activities — their spiritual life, their school life, and their home life. What more can I ask in the name of closeness?*
2. *In order to do what they want, I have to be totally devoted to our family. I can't get so tired I can't attend church (I hardly ever miss anyway). I need to be organized so I'm free to enjoy them when they get home from school. I need to get our dinner started earlier to be able to relax in the afternoons.*

Hmmm...sounds like I have to lay down my life for our little guys. If I wind up with unappreciative, spoiled brats, then I'm wrong. If I end up with children who will "rise up and call me bless-ed"(Proverbs 31:28), I'll know I did exactly what God has called me to do. I only have one chance at it. I'm choosing to lay down my life. I pray it's the right choice.

Somehow, deep in my spirit, I believe it is.

The scene I just described didn't show all that was behind the curtain. Often the children had needs that weren't evident without discussion, probing, and the discernment that only God could provide. This wasn't a quick process. I continuously resolved to be a better time manager so I could be flexible enough to have time to understand — and enjoy — my children. The weekend following the dumbwaiter episode showed more of my struggles.

September 26, 1981
Dear Journal,

Yesterday was Saturday. My back hurt. Made me wonder if something was really wrong with me. Sometimes I worry about how I would cope if I ever got really sick. The hardest thing would be sitting around, seeing things that weren't getting done. At times like this, the boys' messy habits look a lot worse to me, and I imagine how the house would look if I didn't have Emma to help and she and I didn't clean behind them. I wonder if other mothers ever feel this way. Maybe that's what keeps us going — feeling we can't be replaced!

Today I was determined to make it to Sunday school, since Burt was teaching. I tried, but realizing it would make us late, he went on and I stayed behind to finish dressing Clint and Josh. Besides, Josh is potty training himself (at 2 yrs., 3 months), and I didn't want to leave him too long in the nursery until he was free of accidents. Also, he's learning to sit in church with us, so I didn't want to push him too hard this morning before we got to church.

Well, I dressed him three times! First the hand-me-down outfit was too big; then I dressed him all cute and he went outside and played in the dirt; then he wet his training pants, and I had to start all over. We gave up Sunday school altogether.

I wonder if I'll always remember the frustration of Sunday mornings: the last minute dirty diapers, Sunday clothes that often didn't fit (because I didn't try them on the night before), the shoe that inevitably got lost, the hassle of trying to fix Sunday dinner.

Will I ever have a manageable routine?

I'm not sure I ever resolved that last question. Will Rogers said, "Life is just one darn thing after another." My paraphrase was, "Life is just one darn interruption after another." Once that was reconciled in my mind, I seemed better able to cope. I came to expect interruptions and changes in my plans. Without getting too deep into the psychology of human behavior, I'll just say that coping with interrupted schedules is more difficult for some people than it is with others.

The important thing to remember is that our circumstances don't last forever. Children grow up; eventually they leave home. Hopefully we have created the kind of atmosphere that conveys to them our availability and makes them want to come back. Of course a child has to be taught boundaries and limitations that are necessary, but the mothering process is more gratifying when we can accept the disruptions to our plans. Typically when daily annoyances such as a spill on the floor or a child's meltdown or a lost item got the best of me, it was because I was tired. Sometimes the fatigue came from trying to perform the way I thought someone else expected me to. I read the accomplishments of various mothers and tried to combine the outstanding traits of each of them and become that woman. Although I wanted to be Supermom, I wasn't, so I had to learn not to set unrealistic goals for myself. Just as we need to know how each child is wired, we need to accept our own capabilities and limitations. For what it's worth, it's my opinion that a woman doesn't come to fully accept herself until she's lived about forty years. (Some can take comfort in that.)

SCENE THREE: BEING SPONTANEOUS

October 23, 1982
Dear Journal,
This morning I needed to clean house, but when Emma got here I couldn't get motivated to do it. Finally I decided to do what I really wanted to do: make cucumber pickle! The notion had never hit me before. So Emma and I took the little boys (Clint and Josh) with us to the field of cucumbers Burt had planted for market to pick finger-size cucumbers. We worked for over two hours. The boys played in the mud, ate the "lunch" I packed them, and talked incessantly.

I had a wonderful opportunity to quiz Emma about how she raised her 13 children. "Did your oldest child 'boss' the younger ones around?" I asked.

"My goodness, yes," she said. " They called her 'Sarge.'"

Emma also said bringing the boys with us to the cucumber field reminded her of when she took her children to work with her. "Do all children talk this much?" I wanted to know.

"Sure," she said, "until they get tired and ready to go home."

I enjoyed this day so much. The pickles might not be worth eating, but the memory of our day will be cherished forever.

I think what I felt that day was a sense of freedom. Freedom from the routine. Freedom to go back to some kind of primal lifestyle when things were less complicated. I still recall the smell of the earth as we explored the cucumber vines, the way the South Georgia sunshine felt on my back, the sound of children ripping through the field as they laughed and chased each other, and the comfortable camaraderie I shared with Emma, a veteran mother.

When I see pictures of women in the old days quilting together I think, "How boring!" But then I wonder if this was when women offered advice, shared homemaking tips, counseled on marriage, vented their emotions, and shared a bond.

Women have always needed connection with other women. Today it's obvious from the innumerable social networking methods. If I were a young mom right now I'd probably read the tips, hints, and practices of other mothers, try to incorporate them into my routine, then beat myself up because I couldn't do everything perfectly. Teddy Roosevelt is credited with saying, "Comparison is the thief of joy." He couldn't have been more on target. Moms, especially, can be slaves to the habit of comparison. Maybe it's because there is no barometer to measure the outcome until our children become adults. Only then can we know for sure if our method was best for them. Meanwhile, as we go through the process, we frequently second guess ourselves because we see other mothers who appear to have the conundrums figured out.

That day in the cucumber patch with Emma taught me something. It taught me to live in the moment, to enjoy being my own self, and do something basic and satisfying to my soul.

A few days later, I did something similar, this time with my two little boys.

SCENE FOUR: THE WALK

October 28, 1982
Dear Journal,

This morning the little boys (Clint and Josh) and I went for a walk. We started on a half-mile hike to the mailbox to leave a check for postage stamps. What an adventure we had! We saw worms — wiggly earthworms — spiders, mushrooms, dead logs (or"yogs," as the boys said) and "weaves." Josh would ask, "Did God make so and so? Why did God make ants? Bees are our fwiends, aren't they?" I loved the excitement in his voice when he'd say "Yook, Cwint, yook!" and Clint would say, "Joshie, are you my pal?"

They each took some of their "babies" along. Clint had his kitty cat (originally mine from my childhood), and two little stuffed bears. Josh had his Winnie-the-Pooh bear and a small stuffed bear from Disneyworld. They snuggled and cuddled their pets all the way to the mailbox. Intermittently they held hands with me, which slowed my walking gait. I thought how I never want to see the day I start out walking for exercise and regret not having a dirty, chubby little hand in mine when I had the opportunity. I know the day is coming when I won't have anyone to slow my pace, when my schedule will be mine alone. I want to cherish the opportunities I have now. I also want to look forward to a future day when I'm old, and they slow their steps to match mine.

I loved looking at their shiny hair in the sunlight, and sharing their delight at every discovery. I listened to the birds twittering in the woods, and thanked God for the peace surrounding us...and the freedom.

Taking time to relax with our children wasn't easy for me. The demands of homemaking often trumped spending leisure time with them. Every time I did, it made me wonder why I didn't do it more.

I think I know the answer. With so much to do, I felt guilty when I wasn't busy. I blamed this on Burt Sr.'s energetic pace. He never seemed to slow down, and I didn't want to feel like a slacker. (He never put this judgment on me; it was my own fabrication.) The most soothing thing he could do for me was to shut our bedroom door quietly when he left early in the morning, particularly on weekends when the boys and I could sleep later. The muffled thump of the door's closing made me feel that I had permission to rest.

It took years of practice to learn how to let things go and spend time enjoying our children as well as indulge in some time for myself. For anyone who wants to be a good mother, finding that balance is probably a challenge. If a woman stays at home, there's the guilt of not contributing enough financial help; for the woman working outside the home, it's the frustration of not spending time with the children. In the introduction of his book entitled *Parenting: From Surviving to Thriving*, author Chuck Swindoll quotes another wise observer saying, "Guilt is a an occupational hazard of mothering."[3]

We simply need to forgive ourselves for not being perfect at all times. In fact, perfection is a relative condition. What is perfect for one family might not work the same in another household. Tips and tricks that help make parenting more successful are good to know about. However, we can place guilt upon ourselves because we do or don't breastfeed, homeschool our children, work outside the home, make our own yogurt, grow organic food, have a firm schedule, etc. These thoughts are like thieves that steal the joy of nurturing our children. Being a mother is hard work. Whoever coined the phrase "working mother" had to be a single college male...or a spoiled teenager. The slogan on my favorite sweatshirt said it best: "*Every* mother is a working mother!"

So let's give ourselves some credit — and treat ourselves to a pedicure now and then.

Taking a Walk

SCENE FIVE: BOYS MATURE (REALLY)

November 29, 1983
Dear Journal,

I feel so much better! There are several reason why.

First, I got our house all clean and organized when I had a birthday luncheon for my mother-in-law and her good friend earlier in November. It made me feel so good to get the silver polished, and the kitchen cabinets and drawers organized. I also straightened up the attic and I went through our clothes. (Don't know what those last two things had to do with the birthday party, but it gave me such a feeling of satisfaction.)

Second, there are such great changes in the children. Our oldest two are so much more congenial, and they don't pester the next younger brother nearly as much. Burt Jr. can sense when I need some help and he will come to my rescue when I'm worn out from keeping up with the little ones. The two little ones are getting along so well now also. They play together beautifully; they only squabble occasionally when they want the same toy. Just a few minutes ago, Joshua was crying loudly because Clint had a truck he wanted, and Jed came and took Joshua back to their room and set up bowling pins for him. Jed is like the Pied Piper when it comes to his little brothers. It fascinates me to see how the younger brothers always look to the older one and want his attention and approval. The other night, Burt Jr. slept with Clint and Josh in a single bed, just because they wanted to. When we hosted a Bible study group recently, we found all five of them asleep in our bed. I believe they can sense the deep love that their dad and I have for them, and they respond by loving one another.

Third, Burt Sr. and I have started meeting with other farming couples for Bible study, and that has made a huge difference in our attitudes. We are in fellowship with others who are dealing with some of the same challenges as we are, and we are seeking the Lord's answers together.

Finally, I have accomplished some of my goals, such as being better organized, and being available when the children need me. I've managed to study regularly with Adam every night, and I've read to the boys almost every night before bedtime. They love to pile on our bed and listen to me read to them. We planned some fun things on weekends, just as we promised them: two college football games – overnight visits with friends, hunting outings, some shopping trips – and the children have responded beautifully. They are so much more cooperative.

A night or two ago, I looked at the toothpaste tube on the bathroom sink. It was squeezed from the bottom. I thought to myself, "That's the kind of family I want us to be; one that squeezes the tube the same way."

W hen Burt Sr. and I were asked to speak to a group of parents at a church once, I shared my comment about the toothpaste tube. To my surprise, I got a big round of applause! It made me realize how much people value family cooperation. Just like a competitive rowing team, a successful family has to operate in sync with each other and pull in the same direction.

It takes diligence to achieve this. We have to first know the direction we want the family to go. If our goal is to be a family that pleases God, we start laying that foundation when our children are born. Actually, we lay that foundation before the children are born. Then as the child matures, we introduce him to Jesus as his Lord, do our best to model godly character for him to emulate, and most importantly, take the time to deal with each child's individual needs. (Have I said parenting takes time?)

Cooperation

We seized moments to brainwash our boys in the importance of being united as a team. We once asked them to help
craft our family mission statement. The idea came after reading
Dr. Stephen Covey's book, *The Seven Habits of Highly Successful
Families.* I don't know if the boys even remember doing it, but
I'm convinced many of the concepts we planted in their minds
affected the outcome of our family and laid the foundation for
their own families later.

SCENE SIX: CHORES

December 14, 1984
Dear Journal,

Today was Clean-up Day. I was tired, the house was a mess, I've been stressing over Christmas (why do I always do that?), and I wanted to experience a hint of organization before the boys were released for the holidays. I called them all together and laid out the plan.

First, finish trimming the tree, which has only been sitting since Thanksgiving. They all had insisted, even their dad, on a tall one — over nine feet. I challenged Burt Jr. to make it to the top. I thought he and Adam would knock it over in the process, but miraculously, the lights got on it and they looked good!

Next, each kid cleaned his room, or at least the space they shared with another brother. In Jed's case, this meant throwing away anything he was tired of looking at, and for Clint it meant re-positioning his piles...but, hey, they tried their best and some of the clutter disappeared without my efforts.

They balked a bit at having to hide the hunting paraphernalia that somehow gets dumped in the corner of the kitchen, but it vanished as well.

As for the rest of the house, I grabbed whoever walked past me for assistance. A five-year-old can vacuum very well. Mopping the kitchen floor was almost a train wreck because as one son pushed the mop, somebody would try to hop on it! Thankfully there were no broken bones at the end of the day.

And I was in a much better mood.

About this time, I started questioning how much to do *for* the boys and how much to expect them to do for themselves. The parenting experts had differing opinions. So did other mothers I talked to. Many youngsters had to make their beds every day. If we had had that rule, we would never have gotten to school on time. I tried making charts, checklists, giving allowances, rewarding responsibilities with treats, taking away privileges...it became overwhelming. I finally came to a conclusion: instead of having regular assigned chores, we just expected them to do what we asked them to. When I needed help, I'd usually grab the first moving body and give him the assignment. (Sometimes it was necessary to get the body to move.)

There were many times in the summer their dad took them to the farm and they worked on whatever he had for them to do. Sometimes that meant pulling weeds in the peanut fields, sometimes loading 100-pound bags of fertilizer in the spreader, sometimes picking vegetables. They often accompanied their grandfather and picked up sticks in his yard, or helped him plant strawberries in his garden. He rewarded them by letting them dig their own fishing worms, and go swimming in their underwear at the creek behind his house. Half the time they were working—that is, actually accomplishing a task—they might have been throwing dirt clods at each other, but somewhere along the way they developed a good work ethic.

They became somewhat entrepreneurial. When our oldest son was about fourteen and the youngest about five, the five of them had a thriving little business selling produce at a local farmer's market. Their grandfather grew peaches, so the boys picked fresh peaches and sold them from the back of our pick-up truck. They added sweet corn and other vegetables to their store as well. Their grandfather, "Papa," drove them to the market, and I'm sure some of his finest moments came when people complimented him on his five grandsons who were working together at such young ages.

IT'S A FAMILY AFFAIR — The Strange brothers of Ellaville, shown above with their father, Burt Strange, seem to be enjoying their first entry into private enterprise as they ready peaches for sale at the Downtown Farmer's Market on Jackson Street. The youngsters launched their peach sale business after first harvesting the fruit grown by their grandfather, James Hart, at his farm on Friendship Road. The youngsters from left are Burt, 13, Adam, 10, Josh, 4, and Jed, age 8. Another brother, Clint, age five, is not shown but is also a member of the sales team. The Downtown Farmer's Market is open Tuesday, Thursday and Saturday mornings from 8 o'clock until 11:30 a.m. for the sale of fresh produce sold curbside on Jackson Street.

Young Entrepreneurs

They made everything a challenge, and it was fun to them. If they were picking something (such as peaches or cucumbers), they competed to see who could get the most. If they were lifting something, they tried to see who could pick up the most weight. Even going as a family to pick blueberries challenged them to see who could fill up his bucket the most times. I didn't have to stay after them to keep busy, oh no. As soon as one of them started slacking off, he became the ridicule of all the brothers. Nobody wanted to be labeled as a wimp or a slacker, so they stimulated one another. Competition worked like oil on a rusty hinge.

As far as housework was concerned, they were generally willing to do what I asked them to. Sometimes in a pinch, I needed somebody to vacuum, or help change sheets, or dust the high places I couldn't reach. (Having tall boys helped.) I

74

never had to bring in groceries, or logs for our huge fireplace. All I had to do was to tell a son something would be too heavy for him to carry, and he'd risk a hernia to make it happen.

The boys came up with their own set of rules for kitchen cleanup. We had a fairly consistent schedule for clearing the table; each son had a certain day for which he was responsible. However, if anyone burped at the table, he would have to do the dishes after that meal. That plan worked like a charm. Everybody was on Burp Patrol. Each one was eager to catch somebody else in violation, especially if it was his own turn to do dishes. Not only that. They carried it one step further. If anyone emitted any other offensive body noise, he had to clean bathrooms. The system was golden. Not only did I not have to be the policeman for sound control, it reduced the number of eruptions boys are notorious for. They even conveyed the rules to their friends who came to visit.

Meanwhile, I tried to identify the balance between giving them responsibility, placing certain expectations on them, and remembering to do the little things that conveyed mother love to them.

October 31, 1981
Dear Journal,

Last night when Adam (age 9) was about to brush his teeth, he said, "Mama, do you remember how you used to cup your hand and let me drink water after you finished brushing my teeth? I used to like for you to do that. I like for you to do things for me like I was a little boy."

I felt bad when I realized how exasperated I used to get with him because he wanted to drink from my hand. I just wanted him to get in the bed!

That conversation made me realize how much some children (if not all) enjoy being pampered at times by their mother. I think I'll have more patience about doing little things for the younger boys after this. Maybe it's not about doing things for them; maybe it's about doing things with them.

I wonder...if you do more with them, would you need to do less for them?

Over and over I'm reminded that good "mothering" and "fathering" means zeroing in on each child individually. And that takes time — all your time! But when a child is conceived, your time is no longer your own anyway. Our pastor said, "What rights you lay down will be returned to you as privileges." I believe in applying that principle to children, it means that investing time in their development when they need it will result in better adjusted, more self-disciplined, and self-reliant individuals. Consequently, as a mother, you will be blessed with more time of your own: fewer trips to the school counselor's office, fewer discipline problems at home, and moments of quiet and peace when they are not with you.

Maybe I'm right, maybe not. The jury is still out for us.

The jury has now ruled. Thank God I was right. Laying down my life for my children was such a small sacrifice compared to the wonderful relationship we share today. Recently our grown-up Adam called me to tell me how his little boy wanted him to cup his hand so he could drink water out of it. Adam said it was a flashback to something he remembered me doing when he was small. Having a conversation like that is like discovering a forgotten treasure. It also reminds me that the times we have to pray for patience with our little ones might be the times when special memories are being made. Having imperturbability in the little years isn't always easy. Many times when I wanted my children to conform to my timetable, they wanted to be children a bit longer. While they wanted to linger in the moment, I wanted to rush through it, stay on schedule, move on to the next thing. Looking back, I see that some of the best scenes took place in incidences when I felt my self-control dwindling.

SCENE SEVEN: SHOP 'TILL YOU DROP

May 10, 1982
Dear Journal,

I felt brave today. I only had two of the boys at home with me, getting along really well, so I went shopping for a birthday gift at the trendy clothing store where all the young women shop. I took with me Jed, age 7, and Josh, age 3. I lectured them thoroughly before we went inside that they were to behave themselves while I shopped. They vowed to be sweeter than angels. But somehow, when they got inside and saw all the clothes dangling temptingly from the rods, and the neat little nooks and crannies which made perfect hiding places, they forgot their promise. They simply couldn't resist the temptations. As I perused the clothes and gift items, I ran into an older woman whom I had always thought was very charming and sophisticated, not to mention someone who always seemed "together." She told me what cute little boys I had. She was forced to say something; they had interrupted me three times in our five-minute conversation, so I could hardly ignore them! When she walked away I turned to reprimand them severely, but they had vanished. I tried to look nonchalant and poised as I searched the store, and just as I met the same gracious lady at the cash register, they jumped out from behind the counter and went, "Agggghhhh"!

I was so embarrassed!!

When we got back in the car, I made it crystal clear that I was disappointed (to put it mildly) at their behavior. I told them we were going to the grocery store (I am such a sadist), and there would be NO treats for them AND that they would be in danger of extinction if they acted up. They reacted typically; the sensitive 7-year-old withdrew into a little slump on the front seat, while the younger one was slightly penitent but insisted that his brother "made" him run around in the store. I think he really wanted to make me feel that it was my fault for taking him in there with all those temptations in the first place.

We had slightly better results in the grocery store. The older child was perfectly behaved, wanting to make reconciliation with me. The younger one was a bit less cooperative. He asked for four different packs of bubblegum (which he did not get), took off his socks and shoes, and drug his little fat feet on the floor to slow down the buggy. I saw another mother (of only two children). She commented on our somewhat unique family structure, and said, "Why don't you write a book?"

Why don't I?

About this time I felt a growing desire to connect with other mothers, especially younger women who looked as if they needed encouragement. After fifteen years I felt I had discovered much about cultivating a family. I knew I still had much more to learn, but I wanted to share with others things the Holy Spirit was teaching me. I also craved interaction with people who liked to write.

In pursuit of this dream, I joined a creative writing class at a local college. Reviving creative aspirations and intellectual challenges with a like-minded group of people was exhilarating. Not only was I doing something I enjoyed, I was sharing about my favorite topic: our family. People actually seemed to like it. One college-age guy said, "I wish my mother would do that for us." His comment assured me there *was* life after babies!

For one assignment, I was asked to describe my family. I exaggerated for fun, hoped our sons wouldn't take offense, and in 1985 portrayed them as follows:

Cast of Characters

Dad: Age 49. Farmer by occupation; dedicated and loving husband; devoted father; a character of highest quality; a masterful human blend of velvet and steel.

Mom: Age 41. Committed mother; contented homemaker; tolerant of noise, mud, dogs, caterpillars, frogs, fishing worms and dirt; intolerant of quarrels, heavy metal music, TV, junk food and lost shoes. Not prone to lose temper or to panic...without a reason.

Burt Jr: Age 15. Often mistaken for 18; typical first-born sibling; responsive to authority, admired by adults, enjoyed by teachers; prefers company of few close friends rather than a crowd; favorite past time, hunting; phlegmatic temperament with touch of melancholy.

Adam: Age 13. Lively, mischievous; a constant tease; enjoys irritating people who annoy him, including grouchy teachers and younger brothers; popular with older ladies and his peer group; likes a party and making good grades.

Jed: Age 10. Very capable and precocious; highly competitive; craves attention from older brothers; neat and well organized; typical middle child, squeezed between two older teenage brothers and two very compatible younger siblings; a teacher's favorite; has strong desire to please parents.

Clint: Age 8. A mother's dream; very compliant; very methodical; rarely forgets something; always happy, loving; enjoyed by his brothers; loved by babysitters; complete with copper hair and one big dimple.

Josh: Age 6. The opposite of Clint.

Celebrating Josh's Birthday

One of the things I enjoyed most about raising our clan was the freedom to banter with them. In that writing assignment I enjoyed characterizing the people in our family constellation, and I relished the little jab I took at Josh. He didn't take offense; in fact, he was proud of the way I described him.

By this time, the boys were taking on distinguishing personalities. Because I was an only child, I thought everybody was like me. What a surprise to discover otherwise! In her book, *Personality Plus for Parents,* Florence Littauer expresses it perfectly:

> Like the cast for a Broadway show, the members of your family play various roles and must work together to produce a successful blend. Unlike the Broadway cast, however, your family members don't audition for their roles. Couples meet and marry without evaluation by

an experienced casting director, and we don't choose some children and send others packing based on how well they fit a role. Instead, we must learn to understand the cast we have and work with it.[4]

To "understand the cast we have and work with it" is the perpetual challenge for all mothers. I found it to be full-time and mentally demanding. With older ones in school and younger ones at home with me, I saw their needs going in different directions. They also started manifesting distinct personality differences. My busy job was trying to figure out what to do when the story line took an unexpected turn — our family life had become a series of changing moods and scenes. I relied heavily on sources outside my own level of experience, especially books dealing with child discipline, the different temperaments, and nutrition. Understanding those three areas helped me manage our boisterous bunch. Since I didn't have a mentor per se to talk to, these materials were vital to me.

Some things were so practical. For example, I learned if I added more quality protein to their diet sometimes it dramatically improved their behavior. One of our boys was especially grumpy when I picked him up from kindergarten at 11:30, but if I gave him a snack like cheese or nuts, he was so much easier to manage, and the ride home was actually pleasant.

I had my favorite reads, but not surprisingly, I discovered the best resource was the Bible. It amazed me how many verses in Proverbs spoke directly to managing a family. I found it presented a perfect balance in family life. The same Bible that says, "Don't fail to correct your children; they won't die if you spank them" (Proverbs 23:13 NLT) also says, "And now a word to you fathers. Don't make your children angry by the way you treat them. Rather, bring them up with the discipline and instruction approved by the Lord" (Ephesians 6:4 NLT). Learning what that last verse means is a lifetime process. It involves studying the Scriptures, praying for insight, reading inspirational books, getting counsel from experienced parents, learning by experience, trying, failing at times, trying again. And never giving up.

Although we didn't know what to call it when our boys were younger, Burt Sr. and I now know the Holy Spirit was teaching us how to honor each other the way God intended when He created families. Now that our sons are grown, we see this principle demonstrated, but it was a process that required repeated episodes of confrontations, apologies, forgiving, and repenting. We all learned to verbalize our apology, ask for the other's forgiveness, and have that person verbalize his forgiveness. We started this practice when the boys were very young, and it continues to operate among us although we're still in the process of perfecting it.

My point is this: if we are surrendered to the leading of the Holy Spirit and willing to let Him deal with our own bad habits and shortcomings, we will be successful as parents. Burt Sr. and I had to grow along with our children. We read books, attended Bible studies, went to marriage retreats, and cultivated our own relationship with the Lord and with each other. It didn't just happen. It demanded intentional effort.

SCENE EIGHT: INDIVIDUAL TIME

September 9, 1982
Dear Journal,

Many days I feel guilty because I put "my list" ahead of "their list."

A few days ago, my little kindergartner wanted to stay home with me. He just didn't have what it took to get up and get moving. After the carpool took the older ones on their merry way, he came out of his room, crawled up in my lap at the breakfast table and sat to eat his French toast. After a few bites to wake himself up, he started telling me all the things on his mind. It seems there was some little boy at school who kicked him, and some big boy he didn't like. He talked on and on about kindergarten. He named all his friends and confessed he wanted to get his teacher a gift: a bottle of perfume and " a little bear you wind up and it plays a song." He talked about how the teacher had "her hands on her head" when he had his "hands on his knee." (Translation: he couldn't follow the directions quickly enough.)

He and I discussed philosophical things like "life" and how there will always be those people who kick others in order to get their own way, and how we have to cope with them. Clint said the little boy who kicked him probably didn't "have Jesus," but he thought the big boy did.

Who would have talked to Clint if I hadn't been available?

I could choose from innumerable examples of "individual time" recorded in my journals. Those occasions helped form the close relationship I enjoy with our sons as they have grown older. I chose this next one because it's one of my favorites.

November 1, 1983
Dear Journal,
 Josh (age four) was upstairs watching TV alone this afternoon because his best buddy (brother Clint) was sick with flu.
 "Turn it off, please, Josh," I said.
 "But I like 'He-Man'," he argued.
 "I don't. It's really absurd."
 "Then will you do something with me?"
 I thought about the mountain of dirty clothes and the stack of unpaid bills waiting on my desk…but Josh was asking for more than my time. He was begging for a relationship.
 "Sure," I said. "Give me 30 minutes and I'll be ready."
 I heard him run eagerly downstairs and set the kitchen timer. "We'll go to the camp!" he exclaimed on the way.
 Soon we started on our adventure. He was such a gallant little escort. "Watch out, Mama," he'd say. "This is a big briar!"
 He attacked every wild muscadine vine and every rotten stump with a vengeance, clearing a path for me. "Watch this, Mama," he'd say, as he tackled a dead tree to push it down.
 We started down a steep slope, thickly covered with fallen leaves. My feet slipped and I bumped all the way down the hill. Josh was delighted. "Mama fell on her fanny! Mama fell on her fanny!" He chided.
 I feigned disapproval. "Josh, are you going to make fun of me?"
 His tone changed instantly. "Oh, Mama, are you all right?" (The boys always ask that right after they've knocked the breath out of somebody.) I don't think Josh was terribly concerned about my physical condition, but he wanted to make sure we weren't going to turn around before reaching the campsite.
 At the bottom of the slope, we came upon a little stream. "Here, Mama, I'll tell you where to cross. Me and Clint know. Here, right here. I'll help you!"

He took my hand, and I think if I had asked him, he would have lain across for me to step on him.

We pulled ourselves up the other side and continued until we reached our destination. The "campsite" is a big hole in the ground, just deep enough and wide enough to look challenging to a small boy. I sat on the edge of the miniature canyon and timed how many seconds it took him to climb up the steep sides. Satisfied that I was impressed, he sat beside me and engaged in serious conversation.

"Mama, you know what [so-and-so] says? He says "b-u-t-t. I don't say b-u-t-t, but he says I do. I don't think he knows Jesus, do you?"

"What about [another friend]?" I asked. "Are you still buddies?"

"Not too much," he answered. "He's kinda' di-noxious."

We sat there, contemplating the questions several minutes. Josh was so serious, his little arms resting on his bent knees, hands clasped, head tilted. I observed the sunshine on his shiny hair, his long eyelashes, his cute little nose, and I resolved to spend more times like these.

"So, who's your best buddy?" I had to ask.

"Hmmm, I guess Clint."

The after-four-thirty chill had begun to settle around us, so I suggested we start home. "Okay," he said, reluctantly. "Can we come back one day and picnic? The whole family?"

He led the way home. I was amazed at his knowledge of the woods. "That's not the way, Mama. This is. See that knot on that pine tree? That's how you know."

He was elated to discover a rub on a tree that he informed me was "where the deer scrubbed off the bark with his horns."

"They're called antlers, Josh. Not horns."

"I know," he said. "Adam told me."

Eventually we caught sight of the house. "I had fun today, Mama," Josh said. "I liked being with you."

Somewhere on my motherhood journey I learned the value of giving individual time to each child. Since I had never had to share either of my parents with a sibling, I hadn't realized how valuable one-on-one time was. I read about John Wesley's mother who gave birth to 19 children. She made a practice of spending twenty minutes each day with each child. I guess she did something right: John Wesley's preaching provided the foundation for the Methodist Church and his brother Charles wrote most of the songs in the Methodist hymnal. Anyway, it must have been my reading her philosophy that inspired me to spend individual time with each of our boys. It took some sacrifice of my personal time, but I found ways to do this.

Time With Dad

For instance, after school I'd pick up one child—him alone—and do something he enjoyed. Sometimes we'd go for ice cream, or visit the new arcade place. The PacMan game was a big fad then, and they enjoyed playing it for hours. I realized it didn't matter so much what we did; it was the fact that the child had his time with me without having to compete for my attention. This system worked better than I expected. One of their first grade teachers said she could always tell when it was Tuesday, the day I picked up our child, because he was always so happy. We started this practice when the oldest three sons were in school. The younger two were still at home, so we had our face time while the older brothers were away.

I thought the other brothers might be jealous of the one getting the attention, but it wasn't that way. It must have been because everyone knew his turn was coming. Each son knew when it was his turn for special time with Mom, and nobody else seemed to mind. Isolating one from the other boys worked best, because the absence of the other brothers always affected the transparency and behavior of the child being treated.

The same thing worked at home regarding their home-work. I set aside individual time for each child after dinner each school night. Sometimes the schedule would go awry and we didn't do it, but the boys liked it so much that they would try to make it work. We'd set the timer in the kitchen for thirty minutes, giving each boy his turn of uninterrupted attention from me. We'd snuggle on the bed and call out spelling words or check homework or frequently just talk. Sometimes when I opened the bedroom door the next person practically fell into the room.

The system worked well, as long as I accepted the fact that I didn't have my personal time. It was a sacrifice, and often caused me to have to stay up late to finish my projects such as cleaning the kitchen or folding a load of laundry, but I'm glad now that I made this choice. It gave me the opportunity to see what the older boys were doing in school, and although the little ones didn't have any serious studying to do, they had my undivided attention. By the time the younger ones were old enough to need some study time, the big boys had moved on to more independence.

I found another effective way to accomplish individual time. When the boys were growing up, we had a thing called "craw-ly-ing." It went on for years, and was especially important when they were teenagers. What this meant was, I spent the better part of the night lying down beside each boy after he got in bed and tickled his back until I thought he was asleep. Our boys had me figured out. They knew that as long as they told me their secrets, I would stay and "crawly." We joked about it.

We both knew when one stopped, so did the other. The understanding was "You crawly. I talk." Many nights I fell asleep and didn't get to my bed until 2:00 or 3:00 a.m. Regardless of how still the boy was, I would invariably hear him mumble, "I love you" or "Good night, Mama" when I tried to sneak out. Those were treasurable times, and now I don't miss that lack of sleep one bit. On second thought…maybe I'm still trying to catch up on my rest.

Anyway, the code words for wanting some crawly time were, "Can we say prayers?" They knew that request would get me to their bedside, and they could enjoy the procedure. I'm sure their prayers were sincere, but I also know they were an effective means to an end. God knew it too. I think He was smiling during each of those sessions. I believe if mothers take time to stay with their sons during those quiet hours, it pays huge dividends in the relationship and the communication between them. In the still hours under the cover of darkness, we have access to some of their private thoughts, their dreams, and their fears.

Boys have a desperate need to talk and express themselves, but they are so consumed with their image that they won't do it when others are around, even — or maybe especially — brothers.

When I taught high school, teenage boys frequently dropped by my room to share something they had written. Surprisingly, their thoughts were often expressed in poetic form. Sometimes the writings were signed "Anonymous," but in every incident I saw their yearning to be heard and understood and their desire to know somebody cared how they felt.

One more important point: I learned (by mistake) to never, ever disclose the secrets a boy shares. Nothing shuts down communication quicker than for a mom to repeat what her son shared in private. A boy's biggest fear is exposure. Maybe the reason some males are reticent to share their feelings is the distress of wondering if they will be wide-open to the world.

SCENE NINE: DISCIPLINE

June 23, 1983
Dear Journal,
  Today I had a showdown with our 13-year-old. It must be boredom from school being out, but seems the boys have annoyed one another worse than ever! The main one is the oldest, who insists on harassing the younger brothers. Finally today I couldn't stand it another minute. I waited until Burt Sr. came home for lunch, not because I wanted him to punish him, but I wanted our son to know his dad was backing me up, and also because I was so exasperated I thought I might hurt him! (Although I wasn't sure I could; he's 6′ tall and outweighs me!)
  Anyway, when Burt Sr. came in, I asked him to follow me to the bedroom where I told our son to wait. I made our big boy pull down his outside pants, lean over the bed, and I spanked him on his bottom. It has been ten years or so since I actually used corporal punishment with him, but this time his behavior was so juvenile, it was appropriate.

With no experience, I didn't know how to go about "training up a child in the way he should go," as Proverbs 2:6 instructs. I just knew I wanted children who were obedient enough to be enjoyable to me as well as to others. Learning how to control outward behavior without "provoking them to wrath" (as well as myself) was challenging, but I knew it had to be done.

Again, I found help in the writings of Susanna Wesley:

In order to form the minds of children, the first thing to be done is to conquer the will and to bring them into an obedient temper. To inform the understanding is a work of time and must with children, proceed by slow degrees, as they're able to bear it. But the subjecting of the will is a thing that must be done at once and the sooner the better. For by neglecting timely correction, they will contract a stubbornness and an obstinacy, which is hardly ever conquered and never without using such severity as would be painful to me as to the children. In the esteem of the world, those who withhold timely correction would pass for kind and indulgent parents, whom I call cruel parents, who permit their children to get habits which they know must afterward be broken...[5]

Always Big Brother

Spanking our 13-year-old was effective. A few weeks later I was leaving his room, and I saw a note he had posted on his message board. It said, Remember: Be nice to brothers. (Note: it was his last spanking.)

As with everything, I learned on the first child. It's a miracle he turned out well. It was liberating to discover I could expect obedience from even a young toddler. One day as I attempted to change one of our squirmy little boys, he repeatedly flipped over and crawled away with amazing speed. I found myself on the floor crawling after him, grabbing his foot and dragging him back, only to have the process repeated. After several attempts, I realized how ridiculous it was for me, a grown up woman, to be on my hands and knees, trying to catch a stubborn little boy. Several good pops on his bare bottom let him know he had to lie still for a diaper change.

Their dad and I were big on making them offer apologies to one another and verbalize forgiveness when there was an altercation. But Burt Sr. took it a step further. He made them hug one another — for longer than a nanosecond. They said this was the worst punishment of all.

Without a doubt, the single most important thing we did was make sure each son not only accepted Jesus Christ as his personal Savior and understood the power of the Holy Spirit, but that he was exposed to every opportunity available to embolden his Christian witness. We encouraged them to read the Bible on their own, and we took them with us to Christian family retreats, to Christian business men's meetings, Christian concerts, Bible studies, seminars, etc. Regardless of how this may come across, we did not brainwash our sons. We never coerced them into going to any of these things, but simply exposed them to the opportunity and tried to make everything as much fun as possible. They had freedom to make the choice. Sometimes we encountered resistance, but not rebellion. Many times they collected friends who wanted to come along. That made a difference. The boys became aware that Christianity didn't require a person to become a weirdo, dress in odd ways, change his personality, or lose his enjoyment of life.

In addition to the spiritual foundation we laid, we introduced some culture as well. The local college in our town offered classical music concerts every quarter with guest musicians performing. They were small events, staged in the intimate rotunda of the Ad Building. It brought the listeners in close proximity to the musicians, and required attentiveness. When my parents first suggested taking a couple of the boys with them, I wasn't so sure how they would cooperate, but they were exemplary. We made a practice of exposing all of them to as much classical culture as they could stand. I also often played classical music in our home, starting when they were too young to protest. I'm not saying they chose to listen to Mozart over the latest hit, but their appreciation for classical talent remained intact as they grew up.

We did try to be as hip as possible, to be as much fun as possible, and to welcome anyone they brought home. We also participated with them in every way we could. Burt Sr. fished, hunted, worked, and played with them. We attended all their games, whatever they were playing. Often we had extra buddies with us. Was this convenient? Not always. Did I enjoy it? Most of it. Did I ever get so tired I couldn't remember my name? Almost every day. Would I do the same things again? Absolutely.

SCENE TEN: DAY OFF

Tuesday, Sept.20, 1984
Dear Journal,

Today I must go through the stuff in Josh's closet. It's such a job: broken toys, bits and pieces of things everywhere, hand-me-down clothes, certain favorite outfits that bring back memories of special occasions. It is hard to dig back into the past without getting sentimental. The only way I can get through it is to look at the neat room and closet and think about how happy we are at this particular moment.

I've been on a rampage to get everything clean, neat, and organized. Once finished, I will have time to spend with the children. It's a tall order. I look around, and it seems like there is so much to do. Thinking about it overwhelms me, but I know I can do it if I just take everything as I come to it and not let it get to me. I also remind myself how good I feel when everything is neat.

S ometimes I had a day to myself. No carpool responsibilities, nowhere I had to be other than at home. It was at such a time as this that I often would choose to do what many women do that baffles many husbands: Organize. I would pull everything out of my closet and reorganize it. When I felt brave I even tackled the walk-in closet in Josh and Clint's room — a daunting task.

Boys can be territorial when it comes to their space. Once I thought I'd do a teenage son a favor and clean his room, top to bottom. (Notice I said once.)

The top of his dresser looked like the wake after a tornado, so I put all the giblets of paper, random snapshots, trinkets, rattlesnake rattles, petrified turkey feet, and other unidentifiable items in neat piles and containers. The room looked so nice...until he came home, and repositioned everything back precisely where it was. After that I left his space alone until he got married.

As the boys matured, I discovered the time I thought I looked forward to—when I could have my house back the way I wanted it—wasn't as appealing as I thought it would be...because it meant a season had passed, and tolerating their clutter was sweeter than living in a decorator's showroom (not that I have that).

SCENE ELEVEN: BUMPS, BRUISES, AND WORSE

May 12, 1985
Dear Adam,

At this moment I'm waiting in the intensive care waiting room. Dad wanted some time alone with you, so he is sitting beside your bed, stroking your hair while you are receiving a blood transfusion.

All this started a week ago yesterday. I'm sure you'll always remember the crash you had on your Honda ATV. You had wanted one of those machines so badly ever since Burt Jr. got his two years ago. We had no idea how dangerous they were when we got yours for you last Christmas. You called me from Dad's shop at the farm and said, "Mom, I've had a crash. You better come quick." You didn't sound upset or excited, but then, you never do. All I could think was that at least you were coherent and could dial the phone. I didn't realize until we got to the ER what a miracle that was, considering the amount of blood you had lost, and the fact that you had walked almost a mile to call us. Burt Jr. didn't realize how badly you were hurt either because he told you that you had better wash your face before I saw you, and then he went to check on the ATV. When we found you at Dad's farm shop, you were a frightening sight. Your head was bleeding profusely, your shirt soaked. (It was your favorite Polo, the one a friend had given you for your birthday.) We didn't know the extent of your injury until we arrived here at the hospital. At the hospital at home they told us you had a skull fracture and possible brain damage, so you were transported via ambulance to a bigger hospital. Dad rode with you, holding your hand and talking to keep you from falling asleep. Here they could find no sign of a fracture, but they did find a blowout fracture in the bony structure under your eye. Tomorrow the plan is for surgery to fix that.

Many thoughts pass through parent's minds at times like these. The most obvious is the feeling of guilt on our part (especially Dad's) for not requiring you to wear a helmet every time you rode. I must admit to you, Adam, that I felt uneasy when you rode your ATV, more than I felt about Burt Jr. I guess that's because I know you, and I knew you had no fear of anything and would push that machine to its limits.

All the way to here, riding behind the ambulance, I prayed for you, and I knew that Daddy, who was riding in the ambulance with you, was praying too. We knew your destiny was beyond our control. I caught a glimpse of you through an open door to the ER here. You were lying on your side on the X-ray table waiting for the CAT scan. The pressure bandage on your head was stained bright red. A very competent looking nurse stood at the door. "He's still bleeding quite a bit, isn't he?" Dad had asked. "Yes," she said, "more than I like to see." She started to close the door. I had the urge to grab her skirt. "Wait!" I had wanted to cry. "Let me tell you about him. Let me tell you how he likes football and fishing, and doing things with his Papa..." She looked at me with a smile – a gentle, professional smile. Then she shut the door, momentarily shutting me out of your life.

Your accident happened at 8:00p.m. Some friends had come to the ER with us, and we sat and waited for the neurosurgeon to come out. Finally he did, and reported that you had NO skull fracture (Hallelujah!), but you had a deep, long gash on the head. "We can't give him any anesthesia," he explained. "He'll just have to hang tough." My stomach muscles relaxed then; I knew you could do that. Later the doctor said that you were braver than most of the adult patients he had treated.

Daddy seemed especially concerned about you when he left last night. He didn't want to make the drive back home. He said that you seemed teary, and he wanted to know what was bothering you. He said that his desire was to spend some special, close time with you, and try to know you as well as a father could know his son.

Getting to know you isn't as easy as it is with some people. We realize that you have a tendency to withdraw when the atmosphere gets tense or hectic. You manage to disappear with your cat, Patches, or go up to your room or something. With all the hustle and bustle of our family, the need to withdraw occurs rather frequently.

Because of your easy-going temperament, you could get over-looked, and we have to make a special effort to find the time to be with you. We don't want you to establish the pattern of withdrawing from us. You are so easy to live with that we get involved with the other boys and our busy routine, and we don't make the time to be with you that we should.

I know you keep your feelings inside, and you don't complain unless things get really bad. You like order, and not a lot of confusion. Sometimes the little boys really annoy you, especially when they bother your things or get too "hyper," as you say. One time you told us that when you have children, you aren't going to put up with their misbehaving and acting up.

I wonder if you are concerned about the surgery tomorrow. I'll never know, probably. I do know that you were wondering how you would look afterwards. You couldn't look any worse than you did a few days ago. One of your friends almost fainted! You looked in the mirror and said, "Hey, I look rough, don't I?"

Yesterday your sense of humor returned. You ordered five dough-nuts for breakfast. Then you got discarded syringes and squirted the nurses and me. You also got on the elevator next to me and went down when I went up, and vice versa, so I couldn't find you. But then you get quiet, and we wonder what you're thinking.

I think having to miss the track meet tomorrow bothers you more than having to have surgery. Since the meet is here in Albany, you asked me if I think you'll have much company tomorrow afternoon. I realize how important your friends are to you.

As frightening as this event was to us, Burt Sr. and I found it to be a time of enriching our relationship with our sec-ond-born. For the two weeks he stayed in the hospital, I never left him. His dad saw him every night. We prayed with him and for him. We witnessed specific answers to prayer. First, there was no skull fracture. Two, when the surgeon operated a few days later, he didn't find the blowout fracture as he expected. He had been so sure of Adam's condition (referring to it as a textbook case), he even reduced his fee after the surgery. And the eye that drooped in its socket beautifully returned to normal.

Before we left the hospital Adam was playing elevator tag (going up as I went down and vice versa), and the dietician came to our room to see what patient had ordered five doughnuts for breakfast.

I can't attest to how it is with girls, but in a family of boys, there probably will be injuries. As tempting as it is to try to hold my sons close and protect them from pain, a mother of boys has to learn to let go and trust God. Reading John Eldridge's book *Wild at Heart*[6] was affirming for me, although it was released after our boys passed their teenage. One of them said to me, "Mom, if you want to understand me, read this book."

As a mother of boys I had to learn to endure hard bleachers on the football field and in the gym, hot sun at baseball games, hours of waiting in the car for a practice to end, trips to get ice packs and band aids during a track meet—and so on—all with a cheerful attitude because I knew I was my sons' greatest fan. All my discomforts ceased momentarily when I saw my own emerging young warriors on the field or court. They looked like sweaty giants with matted hair and pieces of grass sticking to their arms and faces after a football game, but to me they were beautiful. Those were the good memories I embrace now—not the image of the ambulance leaving the football field hauling our son with a broken leg, or the sight of one of them lying in the emergency room, or facing hernia or knee or shoulder surgery, or prostrate on the ground after a fall from a hunting stand.

There are things I can't control. Where I do have a choice is in trusting God's faithfulness. The closer my relationship is to Him, the more assurance I have in what He alone can do, and that is to take care of our boys. Thank God for the angels He supplies to protect them. "But angels are only servants. They are spirits sent from God to care for those who will receive salvation" (Hebrews 1:14 NLT). Although today they are grown men, I still pray for His protection.

Young Warrior

SCENE TWELVE:
SCHOOL MORNING

November 14, 1985
Dear Journal,
  One day I'm going to look back and wonder what life was like when all the boys were in school. They are now 15, 13, 10, 8, and 6. Here's a typical morning:
  It's 10 minutes till 6:00. The house is quiet and the woods outside are still. Suddenly alarms blare, buzz, and beep; radios blast. I lie there, wishing someone would bring me coffee before I have to start the day. It's time to wake the troops. I linger for a few more minutes, planning my strategy.
  When I finally dash into the kitchen, I am greeted by Jed seated at the table, his books spread in front of him. His hair is wet from his morning shower. At 10, he always "styles" his hair every morning (because that's what the big boys do). "Good morning, Mama. Are you proud of me? Let's cook eggs this morning. I'll cook 'em. You go and get everybody up. Let's leave early today, pleeeze!" he pleads. I see he has laid out sacks for everybody's lunch and has put their names on them. (I admire his efficiency, but feel a pang of guilt because I didn't do it the night before.)
  With the aroma of morning coffee beckoning me back to the kitchen, I start the process of mobilizing the troops.
  I start with the easiest one first: Adam, age 13. I never dread waking him; he usually responds quickly. I push open his door bearing a sign that reads, "Do not Disturb; I'm Disturbed Enough

Already." (Not so, I think. He's about as adjusted and confident a boy as I know.) His room is filled with souvenirs and memorabilia, from the ceramic Bassett hound guarding the doorway to the pile of stuffed cats, most of them gifts from friends when he was hospitalized after a 3-wheeler crash. I ruffle his hair, exposing the big scar on his head from the accident. The sight of it always reminds me to be thankful. The smell of soap hits me and I know he's already had a shower and is back in bed to fool me.

"'Morning, Son."

"Hey, Mo!" He springs up from bed, his outfit for the day laid out on a chair. It's "Clash Day" for Homecoming Week: the day every-body wears mismatched outfits, denoting the clash between opposing teams. Adam gets into the spirit of the day, always up for whatever the peers are enjoying.

"Like my outfit?" he asks.

"Cool," I say.

"Are you bringing lunches for my table today?" It's a treat I do for him from time to time (the best way to assure my popularity with his friends).

"Yep, I am."

"Well, don't be late. And don't wear something dumb!" (He's telling ME not to wear something dumb?! And what, to an 13-year-old, is not dumb?)

I move on to Burt Jr., age 15. His door is usually locked. He wants to find a sign that reads, "No Trespassing; Violators Will Be Killed and Eaten." Until he does, I take my chances. I unlock the door with the screwdriver conveniently located for such purposes and enter the room littered with evidences of last night's basketball game: size 13 shoes, uniform, warm-ups scattered around. I suddenly remember I need to see if the jeans I left in the dryer last night are dry. There is nothing visible in his bed but a big lump under the covers.

"Burt?" No response. I try again. And again. I lean over and attempt to roll him back and forth. Suddenly a long arm comes from under the cover and snatches me, pinning me to the bed.

"Burrrrrt! I have to get up!" It's hopeless to wrestle his gangly teenage frame, already over 6 feet tall. "What are you wearing for Clash Day?"

101

Apparently that question reminds him he hates attention drawn to himself because I feel him loosen his grip on me and sigh. "Nothin'."

"Com'on, Burt," I insist. "Where's your spirit?"

"I'm not doing it." Okay. I have more to think about this morning.

I go downstairs and I find Jed cooking eggs. "Hey, Mama. I'm fixin' eggs for everybody so we can get ready. I've cooked eleven; is that enough? Clint and Josh aren't up!"

I glance at the paper sack with their lunches standing on the counter. I still have to make two more sandwiches.

I'm on to hurry the "little boys" along. Clint is fairly easy. His first grade "sign and return" papers are on the floor by his bed, ready for me to see. (Wish I'd done that last night, too!)

"Hurry, Clint. Let me know if you need me to help you."

Josh, my kindergartener, will take more effort. Getting him to sleep at night is always a challenge, but waking him up in the morning...that's arduous!

"JOSHie! Wake up!!" His alarm blares. I shake, tickle, and roll him. Finally he's standing.

Back to the kitchen! It's now 7:30. We have to leave at 7:50, at the latest.

Such a mad rush: brushing teeth, finishing lunches, checking papers, grabbing a clean jersey.

"Okay, Everybody! Let's GO! Where is JOSH??"

"He's washing his boots," Clint informs me.

"He's...what?"

Sure enough. I find Josh with his boots in the sink in his bathroom, washing mud off the sides. On the floor is a towel permanently dyed with red Georgia clay. I control my outburst, peel off his pajamas, and yank on jeans and a shirt. Forget team spirit: every day could be "Clash Day" as far as Josh is concerned.

Jed is in the kitchen, agonizing over his attire. He wants to be "spirited," but he's so afraid his 3rd grade friends won't be dressed up. "Com'on, Buddy," I plead. "You spent hours deciding what to wear today. It's a cute clash outfit."

"But it's not post to be 'cute'!" he whimpers.

"What I mean is, it's perfect for today. Please hurry! We've got to go!"

We finally make it to the car. Burt Jr. compromises by wearing a pair of mismatched socks. Adam is all decked out, but disappointed we won't be early getting to school so he can socialize. Jed is still vacillating over what to wear, so he puts a clashing shirt in his backpack. Clint is compliant and sitting still in the car, and Josh is gloomy his boots aren't clean. They give me my orders and reminders for the day:

Burt:"Remember I have practice after school. And I have to get this broken wire fixed on my braces."

Adam:"There's a pep rally at 6:00. I'm going home with Richard. I forgot my long white socks; they're in the dryer. Can you bring them back before the bus leaves at 3:30?"

Jed:"Can Papa pick us up today? My music lesson is after school, before my haircut."

Clint:"Do Josh and I have to ride the bus home? Can we go home with Emma till you get back?"

Josh:"Can I have Rob over Saturday?"

We get to school. Burt and Adam always want to be let out well away from the high school parking lot. Burt's embarrassed at having so many youngsters (with the same parents) get out of one car! Jed's "gang" see him coming and wave to him. They all check out each other's attire. Clint and Josh wait for me to pull up closer to the front of the school. Clint hesitates near the car to whisper his last "I love you" before running to his class.

My drive home is slow. I ponder the indescribable fulfillment I feel from mothering them.

People ask me how I do it. I don't. I feel like a lousy failure. I yell. I cry. I fuss. I feel I could do so much better as a mom. Tomorrow will be different, I resolve. I'll get everything together the night before. I'll get to bed on time so I'm not so tired in the morning. I'll bake homemade cookies. I'll remind myself these years are passing so quickly and my little guys are getting so old. I'll remember to be more thankful... and when my alarm jolts me awake, I'll rise and be a better mother.

God, please help me!

F or years it seemed we did the same things every morning, faced the same challenges. I felt I was caught in a time warp where I relived all the mistakes from the day before, but was helpless to stop repeating them. I felt that I was always running behind.

The boys' personalities began to emerge and the differences in their temperaments became evident. Clashes, both verbal and physical, happened frequently. Their rapidly changing dispositions frightened me because I felt inadequate to meet their various needs.

Good self-image became the most paramount need as they ventured emotionally further away from their nest. The frustrations they experienced often took the form of physical combat with each other. Boys are unique in that way. They can duke it out like mortal enemies, and shortly afterward be best buds again. I wrote in my journal…

The boys cannot walk without hitting, pinching, pulling, or punching one another. The little ones continuously punch on Burt Jr. who eventually shoves them aside. We repeatedly tell them to stop, and it does absolutely no good. They also "jump" all the time. Anything higher than they are is a challenge. They love leaping and touching a ceiling! Sometimes they even talk me into trying, then make fun of my efforts!

During this period of transition and emerging natures, I never felt a lack of love or dishonor from any of our sons. I attribute this to the foundation Burt Sr. and I laid down for them when they were children. Too often parents wait until their youngsters are older and showing defiance before they attempt to bring them into submission. That spells disaster. It was nothing but the grace of God that led Burt Sr. and me to the right teaching for training children God's way. We certainly weren't perfect parents, and I definitely lost my composure many times, but the basics were in place. Our boys honored God, they honored us, and as they have become grown men, they honor one another. It's beautiful to see.

Maybe I should say a word of encouragement to the mother who hasn't begun proper training early enough. Honesty is probably the best policy. At one point, when I was tired and not seeing to it that the boys obeyed and respected my authority, things began to slip. I knew I didn't have control, and I felt helpless and defeated.

I called the boys together, and first apologized for being negligent in what God had called me to do. I explained it was my responsibility as their parent to see that they obeyed, and that one day I would account to the Lord how well I honored His authority. I acknowledged some of the ways I had let things slide, spelled out the expectations I had for them, and specified the punishment when these things weren't followed. To my amazement, they got it. I'm not saying they didn't challenge me again—definitely not—but they recognized the fact that I was dedicated to doing my job, which was not to let them turn into little monsters.

SCENE THIRTEEN:
REDNECK FISHIN' BOAT

August 6, 1986
Dear Journal,

Tonight we spent probably the best time with Burt Jr. and Adam (ages 16 and 14) we've ever had out together. A special friend took Jed, Clint, and Josh bowling, so Burt Sr. and I took the older boys to Columbus to look at boats.

Burt Jr. was especially attentive to me, offering me his hand, opening doors for me. On the way home he said how much he enjoyed going out and "not having the little ones."

"They all cry and beg to 'sit by Mama'," he said.

"Why would anyone want to sit by Mama?" Adam teased.

Burt Jr. complained, "When we all go to some restaurant together, we look like a welfare line!"

About one of the boats we were considering, he said, "It looks like a redneck fishing boat." Admittedly, it wasn't the prettiest specimen. The carpet was faded and it had a scrape or two, but structurally, it was sound (Dad said).

We ate dinner at a seafood restaurant they liked, and we let them order whatever they wanted. (Such a treat! We didn't even require them to drink water!)

Sometimes it works to separate the ages, and having different combinations of siblings changes the dynamics. I enjoyed not having to referee the whole time we were gone.

It was a special night.

P.S. A few months later, we bought the redneck fishing boat.

Redneck Fishin' Boat

W hen we purchased this boat we didn't realize just how much pleasure it would give our family. Our fishing trips also provided some of the best memories we have. These times allowed Burt Sr. to have good father/son time, and enabled me to have good alone time. I could tidy up the house in leisure and enjoy siting on the screen porch and reading a magazine. It was wonderful not to have the TV on in our bedroom and not have to think about keeping enough food cooked for starving teenagers.

Although Burt Sr. thoroughly enjoyed having his sons go fishing with him, he couldn't safely manage all five. They also liked to have someone in charge of the meals (imagine that), so it was decided I should take some trips with them. The only problem was that the pickup truck could seat no more than four people. And of course there was paraphernalia associated with the fishing excursions.

Finally we devised the perfect way to travel. We decided the two older boys would ride in the cab of the truck with their dad, and the younger boys and I would ride in the back — yes, in the bed of the truck. (I now think it should be called something besides the bed.) The boys thought this was genius. The three younger ones padded the truck bed with sleeping bags, collected all the toy trucks, tractors, and army men to play with, and they were ready for the journey. I discovered that sitting in a sand chair, which I could later use on the beach, afforded a relatively comfortable riding position. Since the sun made it too hot for daytime travel, and because the state troopers would more than likely have hauled us into court, we travelled under the cover of darkness. As crazy as the arrangement was, I can remember the exhilaration I felt as we left at 11:00 p.m. and drove until daybreak, enjoying the night breeze and seeing the stars. The children played and loved being unconventional, and if the older ones argued with their dad about how loud the radio was, I didn't have to know it. Frequently Burt Sr. or one of the boys up front opened the sliding back window on the truck to see how we were doing. I guess they were also making sure they hadn't lost us.

We laugh about this crazy arrangement now. I even did it more than once. Eventually we got sophisticated and purchased a camper shell to cover the truck bed. Then we really traveled in style.

Once we reached our destination, we stayed in a single-wide mobile home. It had no TV or telephone, and we loved it. Many times the boys stayed up almost all night playing card or board games and the younger ones pushed their trucks and caught sand fiddlers. The window air conditioner was loud enough to drown out most of their noise, and Burt Sr. and I let them know not to bother us unless there was blood involved.

One particular incident, when we arrived later than planned, Burt Sr. and I were ready for some rest. When we lay down I felt the trailer vibrating. I got up to see what the boys were up to. I found Burt Jr. and Adam wrestling on the bed in their room. Their hair and faces were wet with sweat from the struggle. I reprimanded them.

"But, Mom, they're calling me 'Puff'!" Burt Jr. explained. Adam burst into laughter. Apparently he and Jed had been ridiculing Burt Jr. for puffing while he was doing his push-ups with

Clint on his back. Adam continued with some silly song he'd made up. I could hardly keep a straight face. About that time Burt Jr. stood, put his arm around my waist and said, "Thank you, Mom, for being such a good, stern mama. That's exactly what we need." His comment was nothing but a placating strat- agem, and I knew the wrestling match wasn't over. I went back to bed as Clint and Josh got even wilder with the frogs they had caught earlier and the trucks the creatures were crammed in. They begged me to let them stay up just a little longer, and I could hear them driving and whispering, and everyone cracking up with laughter long after I went back to bed.

So why talk about all this? Because we now realize the best times a family spends together don't have to be expen- sive, or perfect. I thought these outings were so rudimentary our friends would laugh at us. (They probably laugh at us anyway.) It's all about what makes the family connect with one another. Boys connect through activity and challenges. We didn't have the fanciest fishing tackle or the most impressive boat. Nobody cared. And although it wasn't my first choice of entertainment, I went along with them just to share the expe- rience. All seven of us piled in the boat and headed out to sea. Some of us got seasick, sunburned, and cranky, but when we reminisce, these are the kinds of times we recall.

Trailer Fun

109

SCENE FOURTEEN: PERFECT MOTHER

October 21, 1986
Dear Journal,

Why is it sometimes I'm determined to be the perfect mom? Why not just leave well enough alone? Here's what I mean:

This morning I drug myself out of bed and cooked a choice break-fast: country ham, grits, eggs, and homemade biscuits. The boys came in too late to adequately enjoy it, and Dad came in as they were beginning to settle at the table. Adam said he wasn't hungry, only wanted a taste of ham; Burt Jr. and Jed didn't want grits because they only liked cream of wheat (last week it was grits); Josh cried because I put "that stuff" (meaning ham redeye gravy) on his grits. I let my irritation show. Burt Jr. apologized, while their dad tried to tell them what a choice breakfast it was.

After they left for school, I reflected over the morning. What luxury: someone cooking breakfast for you! Awakening to the aroma of ham frying, coffee brewing... are these things merely "mom jobs" that everybody takes for granted?

Will I ever get some appreciation?

Regardless of how much a mom loves her children or her husband, there are days we simply feel overlooked and that our desires aren't important. I found often it wasn't the episode itself that caused my angst, but the fact that everything else—the farm, the outings with the boys, the TV ballgame, the unexpected visitor, a friend in need, in fact everything—seemed to come before my wants. Some days were simply designated for self-pity.

Now that I'm on the other side of those feelings, I still empathize with moms embroiled in child rearing and the despairing feeling that often comes with it. No doubt it is the Enemy of the Spirit who seeks to discourage women in this season of vulnerability. Being surrounded by small children constantly is a threat to anyone's self-esteem. Of course she's not appreciated! It will be years before a child can begin to understand the sacrifices a dedicated mother makes. Over time, when God's plan is followed, our needs are met. We moms simply have to wait our turn.

Clearly, parents need to spend intentional, dedicated time with their children during the early formative years (up to age five, some experts say), but I believe the older a child gets, the more he needs parental availability. Parents make a mistake by assuming their teenage children don't want them around. I read that a boy goes through a particular age of vulnerability at age ten and age thirteen. Maybe so. Personally, I think every age is open to attack, and parents have to be vigilant to detect the presence of the enemy. The more available a parent is to listen without making the child feel he's a nuisance or an intrusion, the more he will open up.

Of course a busy mother or dad can't neglect duties associated with successful living. But we can put down our magazine, turn off the television (technological innovations make it possible to watch the ballgame's ending in delayed time), close the computer, or silence the phone when a child needs to talk.

However, a child needs to know he's not to interrupt every conversation or demand mom to stop something important just to cater to his whims. This is a different issue, a part of training a child to be respectful. A mom's role might be that of serving, but the child should never treat her as a servant. (Hmmm…that's a ponderable thought.)

SCENE FIFTEEN:
SEASON OF LIFE

July 19, 1989
Dear Journal,

It's now 11:00 p.m. Today was our 20th wedding anniversary. It didn't exactly turn out the way I expected it to. Burt had a surprise up his sleeve: he had made reservations at some mysterious, romantic place we'd never been before. I envisioned myself in a chic black dress, being escorted to a linen-draped table in a candlelight setting. I looked forward to being able to finish a conversation.

The only problem was Clint's little league all-star team won their game yesterday, and had to return to Fitzgerald (a two-hour drive from home) to play again this afternoon. We missed the game yesterday because Burt Sr. had taken all the other boys to South Carolina for an overnight fishing trip and didn't get back until this morning. Clint, his friend, and I stayed at Mom's house and the boys rode with the friend's parents to yesterday's game. Burt and I felt we needed to support Clint and his team today, so while we were eating dinner at a small chain steakhouse in South Georgia, Burt called the "mystery place" and cancelled our reservations.

We're now in the car on our way back after the game. Our anniversary was shared with a happy little boy. Clint has been pleasant company on our ride home. I commented on it being our anniversary and he finished my thought by saying, "...and you spent it watching your son play baseball."

I'm so glad we did.

Throughout this season of child tending I accepted the fact that my needs would have to wait. Once I became reconciled with this, I began to enjoy our family even more, even when we spent several years celebrating our July wedding anniversary sitting on hard bleachers facing the hot afternoon sun, cheering our Little League All-star Team on to victory. We shared many anniversary dinners at fast food restaurants after a game, and many anniversary nights I stayed up late trying to eradicate red Georgia clay stains from white uniforms.

Our boys' summer breaks involved constant family activities, and after a few adjustments we always fell into a routine. I helped them cut broccoli to take to the Farmer's Market, along with the peaches and corn their grandfather grew. They frequently went to the field with Burt Sr., and now they were old enough to drive farm equipment and actually help him. Sometimes it seemed all I did with my time was prepare meals and wash clothes. We moms don't get accolades for services like these, but we take comfort in knowing it's the investment we make for future returns. In my case, the blessings have returned one hundredfold.

SCENE SIXTEEN: CHRISTMAS AT OUR HOUSE

December 31, 1989
Dear Journal,

Inevitably, people ask the question, "What's Christmas like at your house?" I find myself wanting to give them a really impressive answer, describing the tradition and ceremony we perfect every year. In reality, what I find at the top of my mental New Year's resolution list are determinations that pertain to the next Christmas season. I resolve to shop earlier, bake more, be more creative with gifts for friends. I look at all the Christmas magazines (which I didn't have time to read before the holidays), and see all the clever tricks I could have done if I'd had the time.

I wonder what the children think of me. I fear they see me disorganized, tired, running to keep pace with everybody else, who seem to be gliding seamlessly along.

On Christmas Eve I asked Burt Jr. if he liked Christmas the way we did it. "I love it!" he responded so emphatically I was taken aback. "I really like the way ya'll hide our presents," he went on. He was referring to our habit of putting all the boys' presents in the most creative hiding places we can think of.

Somehow we never became traditionalists, as far as Santa Claus is concerned. Because hiding presents became such fun, the Santa game was unnecessary. This year I managed to get some of their gifts wrapped ahead of time, and I put them under the tree for effect. The boys saw them, and someone exclaimed in dismay, "You mean, you

114

aren't going to hide them?" I assured them nothing would be in sight on Christmas morning.

The weekend before Christmas this year, one of our favorite babysitters came home from college for the holidays. She volunteered to stay with the boys so Burt Sr. and I could get away by ourselves. We left for an overnight trip to finish our shopping.

Upon our return, the instant we stopped the car, the front door flung open and out poured all five boys and the babysitter running ahead of each other, all talking at once. It took us a minute to get their message in the ruckus.

"Mom! Dad! Bud (our dog)...guess what he did? He peed on the tree!"

The boys went into convulsive laughter while the bird dog now sat like a stone statue on the front porch as if wondering what all the fervor was about. I wanted to be mad with him for getting in the house in the first place, not to mention claiming the tree as his territory! But because the boys thought the incident was so hilarious, I couldn't stay angry for long.

On Christmas Eve, one of the boys was helping me carry gifts from our house to their grandmother's, where we always go for oyster stew and crab bisque. I lamented to him how I wish I could get things done ahead of time like everybody else seemed to do. He laughed and said, "Mom, you bust your can and you still stay behind, don't you?"

For some reason, that comment eased my condemnation of myself. For someone to recognize I did "bust my can" made me feel better. Sometimes I wondered if anybody ever noticed I actually tried to be efficient. Although I censured myself for the things I didn't do, Christmas Day always came together. The gifts always got hidden. The boys always had fun, even when friends called late in the day to see what they got, and they had to admit they were still looking for their gifts. I can only imagine the puzzled look the friends must have had.

Hiding and seeking the gifts made it seem like they got more than they actually did. They enjoyed each other's discoveries, and it kept them entertained for a long time. The disadvantage was, on occasion, I forgot where we hid some of their presents. I know I should have written it all down, but that called for another step of organization. Sometimes a gift would appear several days later, like the time I hid a huge box of crayons on top of a lamp and the things melted into one big blob.

When we began parenting, Burt Sr. and I didn't know how important traditions were to children. We simply did what seemed expedient for us at the time, and if it worked, Behold! A new tradition was born. The habit of hiding gifts took on a new meaning the first Christmas after my father passed away. We expected a certain sadness to prevail, as it always does the first special occasion without a family member, so we got creative. That year we had rare freezing temperatures in the teens, and the pond behind our house was covered in thick ice. Not only did we hide some gifts around the house, we put the most special ones in trash bags and slid them across the ice. The boys had to use their casting rods to catch the bags and reel them to the bank. Of course they didn't know what was in the bags, so if they reeled in a brother's gift, they tried to see how far they could skim it back across the ice. This was definitely one of our more interesting Christmas searches. And yes, some of them did attempt to walk across the ice to get a bag, and yes, the ice did crack. I'm just thankful they didn't all end up with pneumonia.

In most three-act plays, there is an intermission before the third act. Not in our situation. As the boys morphed into pre-adolescence and teenage, I had no time to relax or prepare for the teenage finale. If anything, it felt like we were just getting ready to go on stage. I watched our boys' evolution, and realized the real show was yet to come — the years they'd have their independence as they started to separate from us. All we could do at this point was stand in the wings and watch them on the stage of Maturity. Were they ready? Would they know their lines without us there to prompt them?

Their individualism was evident. Strengths as well as weaknesses were more recognizable. It was a wild adventure, wonderful and scary at the same time. The scariest thing was the

Gift Hunting

rate at which they were changing. One day they were all little, playing games on the floor together; the next time I looked, we had a high school senior. This phase of life became the most challenging of all. Not that we had rebellious teenagers; they were wonderful guys. The challenge came from the diversity of life stages: one soon to enter college, one entering junior high, one beginning first grade. As close in age as they seemed to be while young, they now appeared to be separated by generations of differences.

As our boys entered adolescence, teenage, and pre-manhood, I felt the need to connect with them in a different way. When they were at school I suddenly felt isolated from them. I found myself trying to find ways to stay in touch. This was God's way of preparing me to do something I never expected: return to teaching.

My first venture was to become a substitute teacher in the school all our sons attended. The next season of our family life revolved around this arrangement.

As you will see, being in the same world as the boys provided opportunities I would never have had otherwise.

ACT III

THE TEEN STAGE

A wise child brings joy to a father…
Proverbs 10:1 (NLT)

SCENE ONE: CHANGES

August 26, 1986
Dear Journal,
If the first day after school is out for summer is the hardest for me, then the second hardest is the day before school starts back... but for different reasons. This time, I've gotten accustomed to their presence at home and the things I associate with summer: the noise, the interruptions, the squabbles, the appetites, the wonderful vacations at the beach.

Now I don't want to let the boys go away from me. I feel they're in a different world. I also feel the kite string of their lives having to be lengthened. I know soon I'll have to release it altogether, and that makes me sad. Especially when I realize Burt Jr. will be a senior this year. Jed will be in the sixth grade, and that's a transition time for him. Josh is in first grade. When did all this time pass?

I'm writing this tonight, the end of the first day. Before going to bed tonight, Jed checked, then rechecked, his school supplies about fifteen times. Clint went to sleep crying because we have found he has a hernia and he's so upset. Before he went to sleep, he put his little head on my chest and asked me to "pray it will all be better." This just about tore my heart out. [Note: it did go away and he never had to have surgery. Praise God for answered prayer!]

I took the boys to school this morning, and as usual, things leveled out. They immediately connected with their friends, and optimism returned. One of Clint's little friends had cried the night before (his mother told me) because she made out the check wrong for his meal ticket; he didn't want to be "fussed at by the teacher."

Burt Jr. had a minor traffic accident and had to go to traffic court (since it was his fault and he was a young driver). Needless to say, he was not very happy about that. The headmaster had to call his name over the intercom when I went by the school office to let him know what time to appear. I wondered if it would embarrass him.

I met a friend for breakfast after dropping them at school, but nothing to eat appealed to me. I needed to run errands, but I didn't have the heart for it. Besides, the boys needed socks and gym shorts washed, and since I don't have any household help any more, it's up to me...and I'm always behind! So I went home.

I drove back slowly, listening to Dr. James Dobsen on the radio as he discussed "letting go" of our children as they get older. I found myself wondering who it's harder on — the child or the parent. Just as in the birth, there is pain involved. I'm feeling the initial emotional pain, knowing the emergence into a bigger world is coming for our sons. The difference is, with the birth of a baby, the mother knows her life is changing and she is getting a new role to play, but she's the main part of the action. As the new little character develops, she becomes more of a backup. It's hard to accept that.

I wasn't the only mother who felt this way today. (This is comforting!) There were many mothers with long faces, several with tears as they let go of their kindergartener's hand. I felt their pain, but I hurt more for my high school senior. It sounds good to say my child is enrolled in such-and-such university, but in my heart I wonder how he'll be on his own. It seems we've just reached the point of talking on a deep level, and he even asks for my opinion. He seems to be testing his emotional wings. I don't want to send him away prematurely!

Anyway, I came home, tried to neaten the house, but I was drained of energy. I finally managed to wash sheets (two wet beds this morning), and socks and underwear. I still have a mountain of laundry facing me.

Two o'clock finally came, and I went back to school to pick up the younger children. The weather was so hot! They got in the car red-faced and sweaty. The youngest two were arguing over whether Clint could go to the birthday party that Josh's friend invited them both to. They fussed until I threatened to make them ride home every day on the school bus! A trip by Wendy's for a "frostie" changed the moods considerably. They sat in the car eating it while I shopped for groceries. When I went back at 3:00 for Jed and Adam, everybody was congenial. Back at home, Clint and Josh immediately checked on their turtles and bullfrog, then started fishing and jumping on the trampoline. They all helped bring in the groceries and put them away.

We had a roast for supper, and when we got together around 7:00 p.m., Dad was home from the field, and Burt Jr. entertained us with stories about his day at court. He was in a jovial mood. He and a friend had played basketball and worked out in the gym for three hours after school. They also had gone to a store and found a lunch box with a radio in it. They thought it would be hilarious to take it to the school lunchroom. He was so hyped up. "This year's going to be a ball," he bragged. "I'm a big senior now! I can do anything!"

Okay, so "senioritis" has hit already. That's fine. I love his spunk!

I regarded our household as a study in human behavior, but the college courses I took on the subject had little relevance to being in the trenches with a bunch of boisterous, hormonal males. I also realized the age differences alone didn't cause all the clashes, but another factor contributed: temperament dissimilarities. Thankfully I found a resource in the writings of Dr. Tim and Beverly LaHaye, who wrote several books on the subject of temperaments.

I analyzed each of our family members and carefully studied the behavior of each son as well as their dad to try to understand why they acted as they did. It helped greatly. As they became interested in the subject, I read them the descriptions of each temperament's strong and weak points. We tried to accent the positive qualities, and we prayed over the negative ones. This understanding made a huge difference in our family relationships. As the boys developed into adulthood, they gradually came to embrace the differences in one another and learn how to use those attributes to work together rather than push against each other. We don't have a family without conflicts, but we learned to mitigate our differences and all row in the same direction. This still challenges us, but we continue to try.

For the first time, I found myself in a quiet house for a few hours every day. My thoughts turned to them in school. What were they doing? Who were their friends? Where did they sit in the lunchroom?

These thoughts birthed in me the desire to go back into the classroom.

SCENE TWO: MAKING FRIENDS WITH FRIENDS

August 26, 1987
Dear Journal,

I'm practicing what a friend told me about getting my sons' friends to like me. First, they had to get to know me. I chose the quickest and most direct route to that end: substitute teaching in our sons' school. I signed up for it this past year.

The first morning I was called to come in was amusing. All the boys had to approve my appearance. Our oldest son was concerned about my decision to become involved at school. I knew in my heart it would work because I taught high school before we had our family, and the fifteen years I stayed at home parenting our sons made me better able to relate to their peers, so I re-entered the classroom with more wisdom and complete confidence. I also found I had missed association with teenagers, so getting back in the teaching mode was an adrenaline high for me.

One morning I was called to sub for a teacher who was in charge of the homeroom of our oldest son. We had agreed earlier that I would say "no" to subbing in one of his classes, but I figured I couldn't do too much damage in a fifteen-minute homeroom period. (Could I?)

So the first homeroom duty at school is to check attendance. It's a dead giveaway that the teacher doesn't know the students if she "calls roll." That just isn't cool. Knowing this, I surreptitiously scanned the room and counted heads. When I looked up, my sweet senior son, from the back row, mouthed the words "nobody's out." It touched *my heart in a place that had never been touched. In that moment, I realized it wasn't because he was embarrassed for me to be seen at school; he was looking out for me! He didn't want the teenagers to think I didn't know them.*

Later in the year, he became comfortable with my presence and I did fill in for one of his teachers. One afternoon he came by my room after school, bent his 6'6" frame over my desk and said, "Mom, everybody enjoyed having you here today. They've been saying how much fun you are!"

I'll never have a finer moment.

I knew in order to stay in touch with my growing men I had to do it on their terms and in their worlds. A wise friend, mother of four, made a comment that shaped my parenting. She said, "See to it your child's friends like you. Then your child almost has to." I found out this was as easily done as said. Substitute teaching opened the door and gave me access into our boys' matrix. It helped me understand them much better; hopefully, it made me a better mother.

Besides substitute teaching, I found other ways to get to know our children's buddies. One good way was to be a driver. They always needed drivers to get them places. The first time I drove to an out-of-town track meet, our station wagon was loaded with eight seventh-grade boys, snacks, and coolers. Our son was both surprised and pleased when it seemed everybody wanted to ride with him. The night before, I relieved his mind of his biggest worry: I promised I would let them choose the radio station.

SCENE THREE: GETTING TO KNOW YOU

March 7, 1988
Dear Journal,

Being at school this year is the best decision I could have made! I feel so connected with the boys — getting to know their friends, seeing what their life is like away from the home setting. I know I am supposed to be here! I've enjoyed watching the changes taking place in the teenagers as they develop into men.

The satisfaction of doing something that makes me feel valued is rewarding as well. For sixteen years I felt I hadn't done anything but change diapers, make pancakes, and attend basketball games.

This morning, however, I feel restless and disoriented. I think it's that I'm trying to come down from the adrenalin high I felt during basketball season. It has been such an emotionally packed time for us. Now that it's over, I am facing a reality: our oldest son is going to graduate and leave home. When I think about it, my stomach hurts and I feel tears forming.

Losing the game in the second round of state finals was such a heartbreaker. I'm still trying to process my emotions. I never dreamed it would affect me this way. I rode back from the game with Burt Jr., who was silent almost all the way. When we got home, he sat in the car, hands on the steering wheel, and said in a subdued voice, "Mom, I just played my last high school game." That's when the reality hit me. It was sad to think of having to wash his uniform to turn it in. I left it in his gym bag from Thursday night until Sunday afternoon.

I substituted at school on Friday. Being there with the high school students who had watched the four seniors play their last game was comforting. After school I bought two dozen doughnuts and three gallons of milk for Burt Jr. and whatever friends might come by over the weekend.

On Saturday, Jed had a Jr. Pro basketball game. Burt Jr. was sweet enough to go to the game to see Jed and his friends play. Jed told me later when Burt Jr. got in the huddle and gave them the "Win!" charge, they got "all pumped up." (Nothing like a big brother to inspire!) Sunday afternoon, Burt Jr. took Clint and Josh and friends of theirs skating.

Today I have been substituting for Burt Jr.'s English class. He was fine with that. (We've come a long way!) During study hall, one of the senior boys pulled his desk close to mine and asked, "What's Burt going to do next year?"

That was the question I heard all day. I had listened to "college talk" since the first bell rang. It was a full-blown impact to realize Southland Academy would no longer be the same without this group of seniors. Suddenly I realized how much I'd miss them. As with other things in life, we don't value them as much until we realize we're about to lose them. I'll not only miss Burt Jr., I'll miss his friends. I can't help but wonder if I've left things undone and unsaid.

Wonder if I'll cry at graduation...?

That year before I finished substitute teaching, it was confirmed: youngsters need to know they are loved unconditionally. Some aren't loveable at first, but I'm convinced there's always a reason, such as a broken home, a broken heart. The most obnoxious ones are looking for someone to understand them. I was surprised at how much the teenagers needed wholesome physical affection. I never had as many hugs from both boys and girls as I did on the days I substituted. Before the year ended, I consented to let a group of seventh grade girls have a spend-the-night party at our house. This began a trend that lasted for the next several years, the same group coming back as well as new groups. I found a bonus in having

First and Future Senior

girls here: I was privy to inside information, details boys would never think to share!

Another trend started about this time too. We began having Bible studies in our home. Sometimes the sessions were structured; sometimes the teens were just hanging out. But it wasn't unusual to have thirty people (at least) with us every other Saturday night. We didn't require our own sons to be present, but we noticed they arranged their activities so they wouldn't miss out. It surprised them to see how many of their friends wanted to be here. One of our sons who was 14 at the time made this observation, "Mom, you know these people might not be coming if they hadn't gotten to know you at school."

That summer I really got brave. I was the only adult who took six eighth grade boys, plus Josh, age ten, to a summer basketball camp in Montgomery, Alabama, and stayed with them for a week in a hotel suite. My never-say-never husband was assuring me I'd be fine as we pulled out at 7:00 a.m., my sweaty palms gripping the steering wheel. He was right. It was one of the most enjoyable weeks I've had. I remember the highlights, but only by reading my journal do I recall the details.

SCENE FOUR: BASKETBALL CAMP

June 14, 1989
Dear Journal,

Tonight finds me in a most unusual situation. I'm spending a week in a motel room with seven boys in Montgomery, Alabama! Before leaving home, I questioned my sanity, especially when the other moms who were supposed to help chaperone backed out.

Leaving things under control at home was the hardest part. I wanted to have the house organized, bills paid, clothes put away, food cooked for Burt Sr., Burt Jr., and Adam.

The campers began arriving this morning at 6:15 a.m. My hair was in heat curlers and I had on no make-up. Burt Sr. and I were up late last night, dealing with our oldest two sons. Burt Jr. just returned home for the summer after his freshman year at college. He needed to talk to us and to recalibrate after being gone for a year. Adam "mischievously" stabbed several of his perfectly good tee shirts with the hunting knife he was sharpening. (I suspected he didn't want them to be handed down to a younger brother, and it made me so mad I hid the new clothes we bought him this spring!) To make matters worse, Josh was in his bed screaming because his arm hurt (we suspected an older brother's fault). I finally got to bed at 1:30 a.m. and got up at 5:00. I was mad at myself because I felt I had waited until the last minute, and mad at everybody else for making so many demands!

Eventually we loaded everybody — and all the accouterments — in the station wagon. The drive to Montgomery went smoothly. The boys were all so compliant and seemed comfortable about going into a new situation, although I did overhear someone ask if anybody was nervous about camp.

I put them out at the college gym and went to Hardee's for biscuit and coffee. Sitting there by myself, reading a magazine, with no one making any demands of me was bliss! I felt responsibility like a big, heavy cape gently sliding off my shoulders. By the time I went back to pick up the boys, I was feeling refreshed and self-assured. After their showers, we went to the mall for ice cream. While the older boys explored the area, Josh and I visited a toy store and a pet shop. It was a rare moment I could be with him and not feel rushed.

The next night Josh begged me to come early to pick them up so I could watch them practice. As the week went on, they all wanted me there. I went, sat on the side and read a book while they played. It didn't bother me to be the only female in the gym with 63 sweating boys. (I counted 'em!) Living in a household of men has had its influence on me. Occasionally I'd see one of my boys looking to catch my eye when he made a commendable shot.

The highlight of the week was watching them ice skate (or attempt to) at the rink inside the mall. I laughed so hard I couldn't catch my breath. As silly as it was, they all dressed alike: camp tee shirts, khaki shorts, white socks and Sebagos. They also purchased and wore college logo caps, becoming even more conspicuous.

They approached the ice with caution (nobody knew how to ice skate), but in ten minutes, they were all slipping and falling, hysterical with laughter. They skated for two hours. Back in the room, we sat up until 4:00 a.m., and they let me listen to their opinions of girls, teachers, and parents. They recognized pretentiousness and façade, and didn't mind volubly analyzing someone's character.

It's now the end of the week, and they're already planning next year's trip to camp, but only if I agree to bring them!

When I realized the other mothers had bailed on me, I first panicked. It made me nervous to think of having the responsibility for seven energetic boys in another city for a week. Having to make arrangements to leave and provide for my hubby and the other sons at home, plus dealing with all the turmoil the night before, I wondered what I was thinking.

However, by the time the week was over, I knew I wouldn't have wanted it any other way.

From this experience I had the chance to observe adolescent behavior up close and personal. For a whole week, I watched these boys interact with each other. I think at times they actually forgot I was there. As I was in the bedroom adjoining theirs, hearing their conversations, I found myself smiling at the things they talked about: older girls, teachers, camp experiences, and what to expect in the eighth grade. They surprised me at their perception of character, at how easily they identified pretense.

The night before we left for the drive home, the boys were in their room showering and changing clothes to go out on the town, which meant we were on our way to the food court at the mall. This occasion gave me a chance to witness what can happen when a younger boy is thrown with a group of older ones. In this case the younger one also lived with four older brothers — and that alone produced a volatile situation. I heard considerable laughter, and then I heard something that sounded like a smack, followed by silence. Never a good sign. My investigation revealed an apparent teasing levied against the youngest member of the group (you know who). Feisty little Josh went for one who was closest to him, nailing the innocent guy with a right hook on the jaw. When I saw the red imprint, it was obvious what happened.

The following dialogue is what surprised me. While I was tending to the victim, apologizing for Josh's behavior and attempting to punish him, the bruised boy said, "It's all right, Miss Careen. Josh just didn't like being picked on by older guys. I know how he feels. I get picked on because I'm usually the smallest." (I'll always love that kid.)

Without disclosing too many family secrets, suffice it to say our youngest son has compensated more than once for his misfortune of being born last in a family of all guys. The point here is to recognize the uniqueness of the birth order of siblings as well as their temperament. The more members of the cast, the more challenging it is. This is why taking time to be away with those boys presented an opportunity I might not have had otherwise. I believe the Lord arranges chances like this for mothers (and dads) to get to know and understand their children. Sadly, we often are too busy to take advantage of those opportunities.

After that trip, Jed gave me instructions to further my popularity with the gang. He said, "I want ya'll to always be in a good mood. You'll always have people around you if you're in a good mood. Promise me you'll do that. Even if you're not in a good mood, act like it."

That bit of advice might be easier said than done.

SCENE FIVE: SEX ED

June 29, 1989
Dear Journal,
Yesterday Clint and Josh were riding with me, and they saw a magazine in the car. I bought it for the recipes, but on the cover was an article entitled. "Sex: Better after 35." It caught their attention.

"'Sex: Better after 35'," Clint read. "I didn't know it could get better; it's so bad!"

"No it isn't, Clint," I argued. "It's exactly what God planned. Sex between a husband and a wife is good. If God made it, you know it's good."

"What is sex, anyway?" asked Josh from the back seat.

"It's what Bud and Babe were doing in the front yard," Clint snickered.

"I thought it was when you got naked and got under the sheets — like the teenagers do," Josh said.

I proceeded to explain it was that, but it was not intended for teenagers or for unmarried couples. Then I pointed out to them we wouldn't have been blessed with them if their father and I had not had sex.

"You mean you and Daddy did that?" Josh asked, aghast.

A few weeks later I had a chance to get another glimpse of their hormonal comprehension. It was in July, and we were at the beach on vacation. Burt Sr. had taken all the boys fishing and they were returning, high on life. Here's the scene.

July 2, 1989
Dear Journal,
    We're at Mexico Beach. It's 3:00 p.m. I was making a sandwich for them to snack on when Clint came into the condo yelling…just for the fun of it. (He has done that a lot this summer.) I was probably still annoyed at being the short order cook all the time, and I wasn't in the mood to listen to his loudness. I ordered him to quiet down and Adam reinforced it with a head-butt or something, which (naturally) made him mad. I was wailing about not knowing why he had outbursts like that when Burt Jr. called from his bathroom, "It's puberty, Mom. You know; he's just having his period!!"

That comment came as such a surprise to me, it neutralized my annoyance. We didn't have girls living in our house, the subject of periods was not brought up in everyday discussions. Not only did his comment cause me to laugh, it showed me the boys actually were going through hormonal changes. They just manifested them differently from girls.

Their increasing awareness of the opposite gender amused me. On the same beach trip, we had good friends there with us who had three sons of their own. When our older boys grabbed their cameras and hurried off for the beach, I gullibly asked what they were going to photograph. They gave me a how-could-you-be-so-dense look and said, "Lawn chairs, Mom!"

It was the same response I'd gotten earlier in the summer when I taunted them by saying, "So, guys, it's summer—no hunting season. What'ya going to do now?" They replied, "Are you kiddin', Mom? This is girl season!"

While the older boys were enjoying girl season, I was savoring the chance to observe the changes and personality diversities I saw emerging in the brothers. By this time, they were ages 19, 17, 14, 12, and 10.

SCENE SIX: DIFFERENT BEACH SCENE

July 24, 1989
Dear Journal,

Twilight has fallen and I'm sitting on the deck at Mexico Beach. Underneath my chair is a Frisbee with four small dead fish floating in a puddle of tepid water. Half a watermelon, minus the heart (the pulp without seeds) sits on the steps, a knife lodged in it. Several pairs of beach shoes are scattered over the porch. The sound of waves gently lapping the shore is soothing me.

I'm fascinated with watching ten-year-old Josh down by the water's edge. He has been there for two and a half hours, playing all by himself. He took his rod, fished for a little while standing in waist-deep water, then stuck his pole in the sand. He played a while, checked his line. I don't know what he was playing; he crawled around on his hands and knees at the waters edge, dug a little while in the sand, perfectly content. When it grew dark, he darted up to the condo, then scampered back to the edge of the water with a flashlight. I thought it interesting he could amuse himself for so long.

Burt Jr. and Adam are inside watching a TV movie. Clint is with them, probably feeling very self-satisfied because he's allowed in their company. Jed is staying tonight with some of our friends who are in the condo next door, very likely a victim of middle-child-freeze-out. The older brothers pick on him the minute he shows up. I hold my tongue when they start in on him because if I come to his defense, it makes him look like a baby. I know it's all just a stage, and the boys are trying to establish their own images, using each other as stools to step up on. They really aren't a problem to me; in fact, they are very sweet to me. It's just there are so many personalities and hormones at work. Boys are boisterous; that's just the way it is.

Each son has his strong points. Burt Jr. has his size (6'6"); Adam has a winsome personality and fine-tuned sense of humor; Jed has his giftedness. I look forward to the day they celebrate each other's uniqueness rather than try to exploit it. Clint and Josh have fussed and argued more this summer than ever. I can't figure that out because they have always stuck together like twins, but I think Clint doesn't want Josh to outshine him. He's perturbed Josh is almost as tall as he.

They are all asserting themselves in some way. When Burt and I were leaving last night to go to eat with one of the other couples, we couldn't find Josh. The children all said he was headed to a local hangout down the beach — the one with pool tables, video games, and fireworks. We drove to it, but didn't see Josh. Burt Sr. and the other dad walked onto the pier and looked through binoculars back toward our condo. They spotted Josh ambling along on his way back, not worrying about a thing. We met him when he came in, tempted to be upset with him. Instead, we told him how important it was to stay with the others instead of wandering off to explore alone. We both felt he was merely asserting his independence, as a ten-year-old is apt to do. We commended ourselves for not reprimanding him in front of the older adolescents. We found out later he'd gone to get a gift for a girl who was feeling left out. (Guess he has a heart after all.)

I am finally at peace with the fact that a vacation for me is not exactly the same as a vacation for them. At times I've thought something was wrong with me because I didn't come back feeling rested the way I'd hoped. This afternoon my friend made me feel better when she said, "You know, Careen, you really have a lot to do, with all those guys. You need a vacation from them!" Having someone outside recognize that was a relief. Maybe nothing's wrong with me, after all!

When we get home, our summer will be half gone. It makes me sad to think about it. Down here, everything is uncomplicated. Back at home, there are decisions to be made, changes to adjust to. Burt Jr.

has completed his first year of college, red-shirted with the basket-ball team, but he wants a change. A decision needs to be made soon concerning plans for this fall. Adam is a rising senior. More changes looming in the wings. Jed, Clint, and Josh are evolving so fast into adolescence. I feel like I'm watching our life on film and it just sped up so fast I can't adjust to the scene changes.

That summer, an interesting prospect developed. The opportunity to teach in the school our sons attended became available to me. After two years of substitute teaching, I had a growing desire to have my own classes. To my delight, I was offered a position to teach four classes a day, so now I became a faculty member and not just a substitute.

After sixteen years of being a working-at-home mom, I accepted the new role and became a working mom (pardon the redundancy). It was physically and mentally exhausting because I had a full-time job at home and a part-time job at school, but it was worth all the effort.

The timing of my part-time career was perfect. Three of our sons were in their teenage years, and the others were on their way. Exposure to their matrix gave me insight into how to relate to that age. It also provided the opportunity to be a participant in their world instead of an observer.

SCENE SEVEN: HOME FOR BOYS

September 4, 1990
Dear Journal,
  I wonder, when I read what I'm writing in these journals years from now, if I'll think what I wrote was funny. For example, last week I had an appointment with my gynecologist. I have obviously been one of his best customers. Of course everybody in the office knew me, but I still had to fill out one of those questionnaires they give you. I guess I was in a humorous mood. Here's how I answered some of the questions:

Q. How many children do you have?
A. Five

Q. How many are living at home?
A. All of them

Q. When was your last period?
A. Probably when I was in college

Q. Are you satisfied with your present method of birth control?
A. Are you kidding?

Q. Do you work outside the home?
A. Yes. I cut the grass.

Q. What is your occupation?
A. I run a Home for Boys!

F inally I felt my life was in rhythm. I loved having my home
for boys. By the time they all reached teenage, I was contented with my role. Sure I was tired, but I had the satisfaction
of doing what I knew God created me to do, and knowing He
was faithful to empower me for the task kept me encouraged.
Laying the foundation when they were small made the difference when our sons began budding into manhood.

When our children were growing up, the following are
some of the values and attitudes Burt Sr. and I tried to instill
in them:

1. Respect for authority.
2. The practice of forgiveness.
3. The satisfaction of work.
4. Honor for the older generation (like grandparents).
5. Obedience to parents.

No, we didn't always do it perfectly. At times we lost our
tempers. At times we lost our patience, but we never lost our
confidence in our boys. We always believed we could count
on them to make good decisions, and we did the best we knew
how to convey that to them. We told them we chose to trust
them rather than police them. They seemed to appreciate this.

Dale Carnegie taught the principle, "Give the other person
a reputation to live up to."[7] It's a scriptural principle as well.
Think about it: God accepts people who are undeserving and
worldly and declares us worthy of being called His children.
The least we can do is let our children know we believe they
are special, dependable, trustworthy, and capable of making
wise decisions. If we have been diligent to guide them in being
this way, we can trust them to live up to our expectations.

When I listened to high school students talking about the
frustrations they had with their parents, frequently their com-
plaint was, "They don't trust me." Sometimes there was good
reason for that, but at other times, I think the teenagers might

have held themselves to a higher standard if the parents hadn't decreed they would fail.

We parents can control outward behavior, but we can't change the heart of our child (or even ourselves, for that matter). This is why we have to have the Lord's help. And this is also why it's so important to start while they're young. As parents, our job is to prepare their hearts to be surrendered to the transforming power of the Holy Spirit. Burt Sr. and I weren't sure exactly how to do this. We knew our goal was for our children to desire to please us in their hearts, not simply obey when we were present. Late Pastor Ron Mehl said, "Our task in rearing children is not to bring about outward conformity, but inward convictions."

When we started our family, the scene was subtly shifting. A lawlessness and disrespect for established authority was beginning to emerge. Parental authority was challenged as it never had been before. Since we were inexperienced and needed someone to guide us in cultivating our children, we sought out teachers who could help us. God used different people to have a profound effect on our family.

We reap what we sow. Now that our sons are grown men, I see the truth clearly. Their dad and I now enjoy the fruits of our sowing. For what seemed like endless years, we sowed the attributes we wanted to have returned to us: consideration for others, tolerance for the differences in each other, patience in learning to understand each other, respect, honor, and appreciation.

There was a period of time we thought we were getting nowhere. The boys showed us glimpses of good fruit from our sowing, but consistency wasn't there. Maybe it wasn't there on our part either. However, after the boys moved away to college, bought their own houses, and experienced life outside their family bubble, the principle of reaping and sowing was substantiated. Our sons now reciprocate the values we established; we experience the satisfaction of seeing these values operate within our family; our children now pass these values onto their children; we enjoy the blessings now that our sons are grown.

Our family was greatly blessed by a series of lessons given by Dr. Bill Ligon.[8] We learned from him the remarkable truth of how to speak blessings over our children. We blessed them verbally, both when we talked with them and even when they were sleeping. His insightful teaching shows us how to declare over our children the attributes we want to see in them. We sow, we bless, we pray, we wait, and we trust God for the harvest.

Becoming Men

SCENE EIGHT: LIFE IS BEAUTIFUL

April 29, 1990
Dear Journal,

Have I said how much I enjoy being the mother of teenagers? There's something going on every minute. Yesterday was a junior high track meet in Tifton. Jed volunteered my chauffeuring services so I hauled a carload of his friends. Of course, it's always more fun when we win! I got home in time to make it to Clint and Josh's little league game. Thank goodness, they're on the same team.

The Jr-Sr dance is underway. Today I met some of the other junior mothers to plan the breakfast following the dance. Later I dropped by the gym to see the progress the juniors were making on the decorating. This afternoon I'm planning to make cookies to take for snacks to those working at the gym.

Adam will be helping MC the Jr-Sr banquet. He thinks it's imperative to get the radio antenna fixed on his car before the Big Weekend. I plan to go with him to Albany and shop together while they're working on it. I have to remember to order the corsage for his date, and have our house ready for them to get dressed there before the dance. All so much fun!

May 5, 1990
Dear Journal,

The Jr-Sr weekend was a blast, just as Burt Jr.'s was, although this time I was more involved because I was at school all the time.

The night of the dance, after Adam took his date home, he got sleepy and stopped on the side of the road for a nap. He got in at 7:30 a.m. and crawled in bed with us. I could tell he had a good time.

Today is the big event Clint and Josh have been looking forward to: Field Day. They'll be on the track all day. I'll be able to watch them when they compete in their events. Yesterday they enjoyed getting their snacks for the day.

After school, a group of eighth grade girls are planning to have a spend-the-night party at our house. Adam and I will take them home with us after school. I'm picking up pizza for supper.

I'm loving this period of peace in my life right now. The dreadful feeling of always being behind and running late — like that crazy rabbit in Alice in Wonderland *— is gone! When I look around, there is order. Things are clean. The sheets are all changed. The shower curtains don't have mildew. Clint's and Josh's outgrown clothes are packed and ready to give away. Their closet is neat. Josh's aquarium is free of green stuff. The refrigerator sparkles; the oven isn't burned. The floor is mopped. There's no cat hair on the furniture. The grass is cut and rain has kept the pond full.*

Life is beautiful!

From the time our oldest son turned 13 until the last son graduated from high school, the scenes became a blur. We spent many hours on bleachers watching ballgames. We weathered the many storms of teenage romances. We prayed over baffling times when the boys became like strangers to us, then rejoiced when they came through that season and rejoined the family. We laughed at their jokes, and we shared countless hours of conversation with them and their friends. We repeatedly verbalized how wonderful it was being the parents of such amazing young men. The boys became our best friends, and if it hadn't been for the few times they exasperated me beyond description, it would have been too painful to let them go. When I once told one of the boys he was being so sweet I didn't know how I'd ever release him to go to college, he replied, "I know, Mom. That's why we have to harass you sometimes."

One of the younger boys expressed the balance we had in our relationship with a Mother's Day card he made in elementary school. On the front he had drawn a red heart (although it looked more like a tooth), but anyway, on the inside he wrote, "Roses are red; violets are blue. You can be a pain, but I still love you."

SCENE NINE: A MOTHER'S HEART

July 3, 1992
Dear Journal,
I have finally reached the place I've wanted to be. I'm sitting at the kitchen table at our favorite "relaxing" spot: Mexico Beach trailer. Burt and four boys (everybody except Burt Jr., who stayed home because of his radio station job) have gone fishing. There is nowhere I'd rather be and nothing I'd rather do than this. Thoughts that beg to be recorded in this journal have been boiling in my mind and my heart for the past month, and I couldn't find time to put them on paper. Now that I have the chance, I hardly know where to start.

I guess the first place is to thank the Lord for the blessings and opportunities to meet the needs of my heart. This morning I read an article in a magazine about a woman who liked to keep a personal journal. She said by pouring out the feelings and emotions she experiences, she discovers who she really is and sees what God is doing in her life.

I'm looking forward to the day I can take all the journals I've kept, put them in order, and read them. I've never done that before.

There seem to be two reasons for that. One is, when I do find time to write, I don't want to take up the time reading.

But the big reason seems to be closer to a fear of what I will discover. Some of the things I've written I'm ashamed of because my attitude was so bad, and some of the things are more embarrassing because they show my insecurities.

I think keeping a journal is like making a patchwork quilt. You work on each little square at a time and then pile them together. Then one day, you take them and piece them together in an orderly fashion. Then when you look at it, it all makes sense...and they tell a unique story.

I'm looking forward to that time, and yet I just realized something else. When the day comes that I'll have time to do all this, I will probably have reached "retirement" or something! I feel a paradox in my mind now. I look forward to not being so busy, and yet I'm afraid if I slow down, I'll have to accept too many changes in my life.

At times I really look forward to Burt Sr.'s slowing down, and to my end of teaching, but then I wonder who we'll be, and what things are going to accompany those changes. I don't know why I entertain such negative thoughts. I've never been through a change that wasn't good.

Like now. The boys are older, and we've never been happier in our lives. They are such good companions. They've never enjoyed each other as much as they have this summer. Adam and Jed have picked and sold vegetables together, and are so different from the two siblings who used to argue all the time. They have all been fabulous help in the house.

Overall, this has been a summer of miracles in our relationships with each other. The periods of time when someone has been out of step with the rest of the family pass, and sunny dispositions return. There is a new sense of cooperation within our family that hasn't been there before.

I thought I was ruined earlier this summer when I found out our housekeeper wouldn't be returning. I was so discouraged about the house, the office, and the tremendous load I felt. The corn was ready, the laundry was mountainous, Burt Jr. came home for the summer after his first year of college, and with everybody in the house, the cooking load doubled. I felt overwhelmed and defeated. Now I sit here with a grateful heart.

Before we left to come down here, Josh shampooed all the carpet in the hall and bedrooms downstairs. He went over it until no dirt showed on a paper towel. He had such a good attitude.

Clint vacuumed upstairs and will clean the carpet when we get back.

They all have picked vegetables, pitched hay, and worked on numerous projects.

Three days later...

It's now the eve of our departure. I enjoyed my time at the beach this afternoon. The boys played "Homerun Derby" in the sand while I relaxed. After coming in, we dressed and went out to dinner. When we returned, everybody pitched in and cleaned the trailer and the yard. Dad, Jed, and Clint cut the grass and picked up pine cones. Josh mopped the floor after I vacuumed it. I just got word, a girl-friend is coming to visit when we get home. I'm so glad I cleaned before we left! I'm getting home just in time to plan Burt Jr.'s 21ˢᵗ birthday dinner.

It's now 11:30 p.m. The boys are back into playing "Spades." They're arguing over who pooted.

I'm going to bed.

Good night, Journal.

Happy Anglers

I t's here I end this story. It only tells the beginning, when the foundation was laid.

Many more scenes come and many more changes occur. My reason for sharing these episodes is to give younger mothers hope and encouragement. The culture has changed since I began my motherhood journey, but one thing hasn't.

The same Lord and the same Holy Spirit who helped me is still on the throne; He still offers divine promptings; and He promised to be as close to us as we will allow Him to be. He is the ultimate and consummate Director for your family drama.

In 1989, the country group *Alabama* recorded the song "High Cotton." One of our boys was preparing to leave for college when he asked us to listen to it. As we sat in his car in our carport with him and heard the words, emotion welled up in me at this line from the chorus, "...Leavin' home was the hardest thing we ever faced..."

Whether or not this was true, they did all grow up, leave the nest, and establish homes of their own. They are now the five happy, well-adjusted, self-disciplined Christian men God intended them to be, and I am eternally grateful He chose me to be their mother.

Last Family Picture Before Marriages

CURTAIN CALL

MEET THE CAST

You yourselves are our letter of recommendation,
written on our hearts, to be known and read by all men.
II Corinthians 3:2 (NRSV)

BURT JR.

(mentor to all the brothers and the real favorite of my mom)

Since mischaracter-izations of my bad behavior abound in the book, I thought I would first set the record straight.

Take the dumb waiter incident that my mom referred to for instance. It could have easily gone off as one of the coolest experiences ever, after I specifically told Josh to keep his hands away from the walls at all times while making the descent. It was more of a case of his not listening than my being irresponsible (which is classic Josh—always wanting to do things his way).

Burt Jr.

Each of us brothers vied for attention. Since I was the oldest, I had a special position—which sometimes was not appreciated by my younger siblings. For example, not portrayed in the book was the role I played in helping to parent them. Like being 16 and the first one to drive was great, and Mom and

Dad even got me a car. I thought I was finally going to be able to get some independence for the first time, until I realized that the car came with strings attached…four strings in particular. I took over car pooling duties for Mom, lugging my brothers around everywhere and having to take the family circus to school. All of this at a very pivotal time in my life while my identity was still being formed. It's a wonder I turned out okay with the effect it had to have had on my image!

Each brother had his unique identity. Adam was always the fun guy, the best joke teller, but also the enigmatic one who spent time alone doing only-God-knows-what. Jed garnered attention because he was the middle child. Mom sometimes tried to step in to defend him, but she finally learned the brothers' way was best. (Whatever didn't kill him made him stronger.) Clint was the easiest one to get along with. I think all brothers would agree. We used to kid him about his red hair (which was really more coppery brown) and his hairy arms, which is why we nicknamed him Esau. We also liked to call him Dent after he let his truck slide into a tree when he was driving on slick grass in the pecan orchard at night with no headlights. Josh…well, he always got attention because he was the cute little brother. I had some special clever nicknames for him as well, although he didn't appreciate them. One time I remember seeing him head-butt Mom because she laughed at one of them. Poor Mom.

Wow, I was and still am so blessed to grow up in the family I did. I'm now 43 years old and still single. I know in the right season I will have a family of my own, and yes, Mom and Dad still want to know all about my dating life and when they are getting some grandchildren from me. The Lord has blessed me in my time as a single man. In this season of my life, I have the privilege of coaching younger men in Christ-centered discipleship by leading Bible studies and hosting Christian community groups. The principles that were instilled in me from a young age by my parents I can now pass along to others who are growing in their walk with the Lord.

I have to admit I cried while reading most of the manuscript, as I didn't comprehend the magnitude of my mom's sacrifice at the time. That she would forgo her desires and make raising us to become five godly men, and the purpose of her life to be a Christ-like endeavor, I am eternally grateful. I look at my mom and say the words to her that we as Christians all long to hear Jesus say to us one day, "Well done good and faithful servant." She sold out for us and gave everything to her assigned task. We are the fruit of her dedication, and she can now enjoy the planting she made in us—a planting of the Lord for a display of His splendor. I pray that my life has the same result, that I can plant seeds as she did and take joy in the duty assigned to me in whatever stage He has me, whether single or married.

Mom said that one day you can be rewarded with the privilege of being a part of your children's lives and indeed that is true. Mom and Dad are my closest friends, and I love them indescribably. My brothers are my best friends. We have played together, worked together, developed and sold businesses together, cried together, prayed together, and ministered together. I am blessed beyond what anyone deserves. As the oldest, I was privileged to have a part in investing in my brothers as we were growing up, which instilled a desire in me to continue encouraging, teaching, and disciplining younger men.

If I can leave a word of advice to parents gleaned from how my parents raised me, I would say to speak words of blessing over your children. Not financial blessing or worldly blessing like being a great athlete or having success, but instead the intangible blessings of God. Tell them things like how you trust them, how courageous they are, how much you value them. Reinforce it by giving them opportunities to be those things even when they fail. The Bible says that the Holy Spirit convicts us in our righteousness. In other words, God sees the potential within us. Even when they fail, let your children know that you see them as they can be instead of sentencing them to be as they are. I heard it said, "Treat a person as he is and he will remain as he is. Treat a person as he could be and he will become all he should be." I believe this principle mixed with love has a powerful impact on families.

I have to say a word about my dad as well, as he was the rock in our family and modeled what it is to love and serve my mom. Generally speaking, a family is negatively impacted if dads don't do their part because they should be the family leaders, and the family follows the pattern of its leader. As for our dad, he went to every game I played in; he spent time with me; he encouraged me when he spoke to me, yes with words, but primarily with his actions. The seeds he planted in me made me the man I am today. Thank you, Dad. I hope I can be the man you have been to us with my wife and family one day.

My life has not turned the way I thought it would. It is better than I thought it could ever be. And it's not because of great riches or success but because of the family and relationships I have in my life. A quote from an anonymous confederate soldier summarizes my feelings: "I got nothing I asked for but everything I hoped for, I am among men most richly blessed." This blessing came through the sacrifice of someone else. First, from Jesus Christ's sacrifice of Himself, and second from parents who were willing to lay down their lives for their sons.

ADAM

W hen I got the first copy of the manuscript I didn't know what to expect. While it was precious to read, it was far from accurate. Mom did pick a favorite. I was the favorite. The other four brothers were good guys—if the contest was for whining or laziness. There is no doubt. I had to be her favorite.

Reading the manuscript for the first time was a trip down a mud-covered, testosterone-filled lane of memories. The recollection

Adam

of growing up together was like a reunion from the happiest place in a distant past. I laughed and cried through the pages, and looking back I could actually see God's hand weaving a story that is unfolding today, though we were unaware of it at the time.

I was really struck by what my mom was thinking after reading behind the scenes of what was going on with her. Many of the events that nearly drove her over the edge of sanity are the events where we have the most vivid and fond memories now. The other four brothers and I were completely clueless as to the stress we were putting on mom. In fact, for me it took having children of my own and reading this manuscript to really understand what the stress of being a mom is like.

There were a number of times where we saw mom teetering on the edge of her sanity. I'm sure it was difficult for her to pick which stories she wanted to include in the book. I remember one in particular where I realized I had gone too far. In our house, reptiles, bugs, and various other animals were always being captured for temporary enjoyment. I went through a phase where I was particularly fond of snakes. I thought Mom would see the humor when I brought one home in a clear plastic can and set it on the kitchen counter for her to find. Watching from a distance as she did a back flop on the kitchen floor, it dawned on me that Mom had her limits. There were many times I was deserving of corporal punishment. Mom just rolled with the punches and kept encouraging us on.

I have children of my own now and it has given me a rear view look at what a pain I must have been. I think Mom was kind in her description of me. Truthfully, I was a sarcastic, know-it-all who had already figured it out. While under my parents' roof, I had a respect and love for Mom, but treated her more like a beloved nanny, short-order cook, and taxi driver all rolled into one. I appreciate and respect her now as the wisest and most caring woman who has ever lived. Now I see that her time taking care of me, cooking for me, and driving me around lead to unplanned and unscripted conversations, many of which I recall to this day. When I was running around chasing my own personal interests as a child, I looked at Mom as someone who was supposed to be on call for me, and I couldn't see the vision or purpose behind what she was doing. Now I see that her ability to put up with me and have an impact on me was because her purpose was to equip me for the future, not just for the next day of school.

Growing up I only knew I had a mom who disciplined me, loved me, supported me, and encouraged me. It wasn't until I became a parent and looked back that I realized her mission was to guide me along a path of love and respect for others and to instill in me a reverence for God.

I was probably the least likely brother to share my feelings with mom. The sharing for me became easier and more frequent the older I became. Now when I think about and describe Mom, I describe her as a woman of incredible wisdom who listened intently without judgment while providing encouragement for whatever I was doing.

Through the preteen and teen years I remember cycles of conflicts with each of my brothers when we really didn't enjoy each other. In fact, at times growing up we seemingly hated each other. I remember being run over by an ATV, pushed halfway through a sheetrock wall, stabbed with a fork, shot with a BB gun, and numerous other limb and life-threatening situations. As we have gotten older there is an appreciation among us for the strengths and abilities we each have. Today I really enjoy time with them and admire my brothers. We were always encouraged to make up and make right with each other. Although in my immaturity I didn't think I ever wanted to see my brothers again, I now rely on them as some of my greatest sources of support. We still love to compete with each other, but it's really cool to know I also have four godly men pulling for me as well.

I'm struggling now with how to be a good dad and a good husband, succeeding some days and failing others. My parents modeled a great marriage and were constant encouragers to my brothers and me. They were planting oaks by the water's edge. Life has often been tough at times, but Mom and Dad provided support that produced in me a resolve to never give up on anything eternally important.

I vividly recall many of the fun times where we were making messes and having a blast. I can also fondly remember the special times Mom spent with me. I can remember how she would sit on the bed and "crawly." I remember what her hand looked like when she would cup it for me to drink water, and I recall times when we were just hanging out and talking. When I look forward 20 years I want my children to have the desire to share the same kind of memories about their parents.

I'm now a long way from the kid who nearly gave mom a heart attack on many different occasions. I'm married to Kellie, a wonderful mom and wife, with two children of my own, a six-year-old girl named Lila and a four-year-old son named James. Having children of my own now, things have come full circle. I see some of the same characteristics that drove Mom mad being played out in my offspring. I also see what consistency and focus over time can do for my children's character.

Thanks, Mom, for staying the course and for seeing that there was something eternally important about what you were doing all those years.

JED

Mom, the first thought I had at the end of your manuscript was to thank you for all you did that I never fully realized until now. You and Dad were loving, patient, self-sacrificing, supportive, forgiving and encouraging to us brothers in spite of our being the mostly normal, often hard-to-deal-with kids that we were. And you are still those same parents today, and I love being back home for a lot of the same reasons I loved growing up there. I don't remember you and Dad preaching to us as we were growing up. Instead, I remember you always showing up for our games, taking interest in our passions, saying and showing us that you loved us and modeling more than telling us how we should act.

Jed

Reading through all of those memories was more emotional than I would have expected. I found myself laughing and crying from chapter to chapter. It reminded me how much I truly love you and Dad and each of the brothers, and that I

161

should say it and show it more often instead of letting time slip away to a busy schedule and endless to-do lists.

Though you and Dad did take us to church, conferences, retreats and other things of purpose, I was reminded that it was simply being together for extended periods of time that formed the basis for building our relationships. Some of the most random times in the margin were some of the best. Whether it was working on the farm as free labor for Dad, being on vacation together in a singlewide trailer, or learning how to run our first business together selling fruit on the street market with our granddad, we always fought and we always grew closer. Also, it's funny how I don't remember most of the frustrations and annoyances, but just the good times.

I do recall, however, the time Adam cut a hole in each one of his old, no- longer-fitting t-shirts as he threw them to me one by one, acting as if I should be thankful to have his old shirts regardless of the holes. I returned the favor by stealing loose change off his dresser anytime he wasn't at home and storing my stockpile of rolled coins behind half empty shotgun shell boxes in my closet. The memory of brothers playing stupid jokes on me (like jerking the line when I was sleeping to make me think I had a fish), while I was miserably seasick on Dad's adventurous fishing trips to Florida, is now pretty dang funny when it wasn't so much so then. It was good reminiscing those good times, and I look forward to adding more stories to the list, now with eight new nieces and nephews and more to come as part of our growing family.

One thing that kept resonating in me as I was reading your draft was how much I appreciated growing up not only in a large immediate family but the extended family that included our grandparents and also the cast of characters around us such as babysitters, family friends, farm employees, church people, brothers' friends and other randoms that always seemed to be around. I didn't realize how much I loved the controlled chaos until I was out of it. Whether it was just us brothers having a heated game of basketball behind the house or having friends over to ride ATVs, shoot guns and go camping, it's the memories of doing things together that stand out.

At 38 and single, I miss having the family and cast of characters always around. Though I've maintained a very active social life, doing life with family and those who gathered around the family day in and day out is different from going to one social event after another. This reality hit me about eight years ago when I looked up and saw most of my friends, and brothers, married with children. I was lonely and depressed. James 1:2 says, "Consider it pure joy, my brothers and sisters, whenever you face trials of many kinds, because you know that the testing of your faith produces perseverance. Let perseverance finish its work so that you may be mature and complete, not lacking anything." I finally started to apply this verse in my life and it gave me a whole new outlook. I know that the work on me is not finished, but I am now truly thankful for some of the trials over these years. It's lead me to change as a person and also to pursue community in a Home Church setting like I read about in Acts 2. Though this community is about as messy as fighting with four brothers growing up, I'm seeing similar fruit and healthy relationships forming. Hopefully I will forget the fights and annoyances in my current community similar to the way I forgot about many of them with the family and be part of a healthy group of people that look more and more like Jesus as time goes by.

Thanks, Mom, for taking the time and effort to do what the Lord put on your heart. Thanks, Bros, for being opponents over the years and friends today. I look forward to the new memories we will make in the coming years. I love you Mom, and thank you and Dad for all you did for us and are still doing!

CLINT

Clint

First off, this is not just a book for women. It is a book that husbands and fathers should read as well. It puts perspective on what a wife/mother goes through, which some husbands and fathers are oblivious to. If a father is absent from his child's life, especially in the first few years, that child will probably be absent from the father's life after these formative years. Husbands need to honor their wives and help raise the children, not watch from the sidelines and wait until they are older. Reading this has helped me gain a better understanding of the responsibility I have as a husband and father.

I'm referred to as The Fourth Son, a.k.a. The Next-to-the-Youngest. Clint is my actual name. I've read the manuscript that Mom has written. I'm not sure how it will impact those outside our family, but for me, it brought back a flood of

memories, emotions, desires, regrets, and many other f(
that make me want to go back to "the good old days.
four other brothers (three older, one younger) and g1
up on a farm with all the land we could explore, I lc
the freedom I felt as a boy. I had my friends growing (
nothing could take the place of a brother. It is still fu
me how we could fight like mortal enemies (especiall
and I) one minute and have each other's back the nex
thing was for sure, if you messed with one of us, you g
in return.

Some of the fondest memories I have revolve arou/
family. We were—and still are—a very close-knit famil
I often wonder why and how this happens. When I look
on things now, I clearly see that Mom and Dad sacrificet
in order to raise us in the admonition of the Lord (Ep:).
They instilled in us to love the Lord and love our neir
(or brother) as ourself (Luke 10:27). We were to honoe
another. It may have taken many years, but we eventuapt
it. I would not trade anything for the way we were raiseid
I am thankful and grateful for it.

I am now married with an amazing wife. She is somuat
of a celebrity; you can read about her in Proverbs 31:12,
25-31. I now have four children of my own—thank You,rd.
As Psalm 127:3 states, "Children are a heritage from the I..."
I now have a much better understanding of how blessmy
brothers and I were growing up. Because of the seeds wn
by our parents and grandparents, I now have a foundath to
raise, teach, train, discipline, and disciple my own chiren.
In today's culture, the world is telling us parents how toaise
our children. It is telling our children how they "deserv' to
be raised. This may not be a popular opinion in today's orld,
but I believe the Word of God stands forever and nobod will
dictate or tell me how to bring up my children other tha the
only One who has the authority and wisdom to do s(my
Lord and Savior, Jesus Christ. As parents, we better be eady
to raise and train soldiers that are ready to fight the fores of
darkness. "For our struggle is not against flesh and blood, but

ainst the rulers, against the authorities, against the powers this dark world and against the spiritual forces of evil in the avenly realms" (Eph. 6:12).

Regarding my own children, I like to look at them as arrows he Lord's hand. I have been given the task of forming them, engthening them, and sharpening them so that they will ready when the Lord launches them into the specific place has for them. Without the strong foundation that was laid my life, starting before I could even talk, I wouldn't have ue how to raise children. I owe a great deal to my parents. I could write books on the memories I have of my child- od. What all of us experience, both good and bad, have an ct on us, and there is one particular episode that had a pro- nd impact on me as a boy.

Let me set the tone: Josh and I were always doing stuff ether. We were best friends as well as worst enemies. We at through a period of time when we fought each other y, at any opportunity, and for any reason. Dad really didn't it, and he tried everything to stop it. I don't remember age exactly but it was somewhere around 10-12. Josh and re playing one-on-one basketball on the best basketball rt that existed...at least to us. It was a concrete slab with relevant paint to make it look like a real court. It had brick ning walls on two sides and a crosstie retaining wall on back. The goal and backboard were mounted on irrigation p that was implanted in the ground. This made for a perfect, instructible basketball court.

Ve were having one of our nightly basketball wars. This w basically full-throttle, full-contact amusement that just happened to have a basketball and goal involved. The object w to do anything possible to stop the opposing brother from scng. (It's no wonder I fouled out of almost every basket- bal game I played in during high school.) It was a rainy night, whh just seemed to add to the drama. I remember it well. The gane was tied and Josh did one of his running-away, impossi- ble-b-defend, completely-blind-luck, over-the-shoulder shots that just happened to go in to win the final game of the night.

Saying I was mad is an understatement; we immediately went into another one of our daily brawls. We didn't get very far when we both heard our dad yelling at us from the upstairs bedroom. He had been watching us, and when the fight broke out he was ready. He came downstairs to diffuse the situation. We were expecting another tail-beating followed by a lecture on how we were to love and honor each other. He was so frustrated with us that I think even he was surprised by what he said. He stood there a minute and then the most dreaded words I'd ever heard came out: "Hug each other; ya'll *hug* each other, and tell the other you are sorry and you love each other."

I didn't even know how to process that. I would rather have had any other form of punishment than that. We begged for corporal punishment over this! It didn't work. Dad made us follow through with his command. Talk about a humbling experience! He said that one day we would learn to appreciate each other and enjoy the friendship we would have. He was right, and it impacted me to such a point that now I have used the same type of correction with my own children. It is pretty amazing to see their hearts soften when they are displaying an act of kindness toward one another.

The thing our parents dealt with was not so much correcting the fighting, but correcting the reason that led to the fighting. The key is to discern a root cause—a sin or heart issue that needs to be addressed. The important thing is to pay attention to the whole picture, not just the outward actions. Boys establishing their pecking order is common and is going to happen, but if there is bullying or demeaning another person, then it must be stopped before it becomes an issue. The more people are around each other, the more there is to be annoyed by, and especially brothers close in age, living in the same house and environment every day, all day long. Parents don't need to suppress a natural desire we boys were given, but need to pray for discernment to know when there is an attitude behind the action that needs correction. The last thing this world needs now is soft, passive boys that have been taught there is something wrong with being rough with their brothers or showing some aggression. I personally think it is good for brothers to fight and banter back and forth, as I believe it is the warrior/provider or survivor instinct we were born with.

I am sure there are some who are wondering, "So how did they turn out?" I don't want to go into what each one of the brothers is doing with his life so I'll take a different approach. Success can be defined as "the accomplishment of one's goals." I would further define success as achieving what the Lord has called a person to do. The Lord called our parents to raise five God-fearing sons. It took a lot of sweat equity invested in each of our lives and because of their relationship with Christ, they did what they were called to do. They raised five disciples, who are now making disciples. That, in my opinion, is success.

I hope we haven't painted the wrong picture. Our family is by no means the model family. This manuscript is not an attempt to gloat or gain any sort of notoriety or credit. There are times I remember that I would rather forget. There were situations that I would love to go back and try again. This can be said of the other brothers as well as our parents. The reality is, apart from our relationship with Jesus Christ, we were merely a family of seven. But because of Him, we are seven ambassadors for Christ who now, along with our individual families, are available for Him to use for His glory. Let him who boasts, boast in the Lord (1 Cor. 1:31).

I've heard it said that by the third or fourth generation, our names, and our accomplishments and achievements are nothing more than a distant memory. My goal is to raise children who love the Lord, and to be remembered for generations to come, not for what I have accomplished or the things I have achieved. Rather, I want my children's children and their children to be impacted to such a degree that I am remembered by the godly heritage that was left and by what was accomplished through Christ.

In closing, as a man, I will speak to men. It's time to man up and take the authority of the Scripture and lead your family as the Lord has called you to do. Love the Lord your God with all your heart and with all your soul and with all your strength and with all your mind (Luke 10:27). Love your wife as Christ loved the Church (Eph. 5:25). Do not provoke your children to anger, but bring them up in the discipline and instruction of the Lord (Eph. 6:4).

Love God. Love others. Serve Christ. Teach your children to do the same.

JOSH

I'm son number five, Josh, a.k.a. The Caboose ...because someone had to keep everyone on track.

Growing up under four driven, competitive, accomplished brothers had its share of benefits and challenges. Survival was based on speed, wit, grit, and determination. It's interesting to think back on my childhood. It seems so surreal, like recalling a movie or reading someone else's life.

Childhood for me was summed up in one word: adventure. Adventure was essentially the barometer that dictated all actions, reactions, decisions, and emotions. The chaos that I read about in Mom's excerpts was the normality that

Josh

brought balance in my life. It took twenty years of life (okay, maybe not 20 years but a solid 17) to realize that what I classified as adventure Mom perceived as stress. (Sorry Mom!) How did I know that catching everything that lives in the woods of South Georgia was not commonplace? Catching the critters was the mundane part; "losing" them in the house, now that was exciting! Seeing who found them first was always an adventure in itself. I found it ironic that the ones who least wanted to find them are the ones who did—like Mom, babysitters, or our unassuming cats. I learned quickly that the tone of the shriek meant the treasure hunt was over and the scolding was next.

My family taught me innumerable things through the lives that they lived out but here are a few that stand out.

Dad taught me unconditional love and forgiveness. Mom taught me what a Proverbs 31 woman is, and what I should seek in a wife. Burt taught me the value of words and how to use them. Adam taught me about my brain and how to use it. Jed taught me about persistence and creativity. Clint taught me about hard work and the sacrifice of losing—which was to lose at no sacrifice.

I remember duels we had on basketball courts that could have been cast on the set of *Gladiator*. We would wake in the mornings best of friends and before the sun went down we were mortal enemies. This cycle continued for years until one night when Dad decided he'd had enough. It was after one of our full-contact basketball games. Calling fouls showed weakness; we were into punching, tackling, etc., and generally trying to kill each other. Literally battered, bruised, and bleeding, Dad called us to his room. Expecting to get beat (a.k.a. firm spanking), we didn't care. We were too mad to feel it. Two scraggly kids, clothes torn and still breathing heavily, we were standing there in front of a disappointed dad, perfectly prepared for our spanking so we could go to bed. We had absolutely left everything on the court as we did every night, but this night was different. As we were standing there and Dad was just looking at us (now with my own children, I know what was going through his head), the silence was beginning to be convicting. In his disappointment and frustration, he rose to a whole new level. It was not until he told us to hug each other and say we loved our brother that the pain become too strong to bear, and we must have matured that night because I never remember physically fighting with Clint after that. I guess nothing will diffuse boiling testosterone like hugging someone you despise at the time and telling him or her you love 'em.

I also remember tying up with Burt one Christmas for scaring him with a potato gun. Now granted the potato gun I had would shoot a potato out of sight, but talk about your classic overreaction…! All I did was stand in the house at the bottom of the first story stairs and call him. When he cleared the opening at the top of the second story, I shot him with a pre-loaded rag charged with ether. Apparently, when a burning rag comes out in a ball it looks like a potato or something else that would cause bodily injury. I can still see the confused look on his face when the FLASH-BOOM went off and this flaming ball of cotton headed straight toward him. He attempted to recoil and fell down at the top of the stairs, only to realize the projectile was a rag that opened like a parachute and never made it to him. He claims his fury was fueled by the fact that it was loud and hurt his ears, but I still believe the truth is it scared him—he may have wet his pants— and the act was viewed as a sign of disrespect, which was intolerable. When he launched himself from the top of the stairs, and his feet never touched till they hit the bottom, I knew it was time to get rollin'. I started running, but I was laughing so hard that he caught up to me in Mom and Dad's room, which would be the only reason he ran me down of course. Long story short, a skirmish ensued that resulted in breaking a thing or two. I was just defending myself, but none-the-less it was the year that Mom said we ruined Christmas…OUCH! There were run-ins with Adam and Jed but much lesser in magnitude, and I don't recall what the reasons were. Most likely the fights with Jed were the result of suppressed anger for his making me run around naked as a child so that I would be his friend. I remember one time, Clint and Jed were ganging up on me, and I took a large bottle of spaghetti sauce and was about to smash it on Jed when I got talked down. That restraint did not happen much as a child; he's so lucky.

I look at each of my brothers and the stages we went through and the times that I couldn't stand them. As tempted as I was to think, I detest them, they are terrible, etc., through it all I realized I would be lucky to grow up like any of them. Truth is, there are many entertaining stories of now-humorous altercations I had with the bros, but there are many more stories of camaraderie and love that make them my best friends. I would say that it's not the similitude of our thinking that unites us, but the respect each of us has for the differences of our opinions. I kid Mom that I was raised by a pack of coyotes because I had to fend for myself all my life, but the truth is, the mother, father, and brothers who left me to be raised by coyotes are the same ones that kept me from being bit. They are the same ones that supported me completely in every endeavor, every triumph, and every failure. I'll never know all the blessings and lessons that I learned from my family but the person I am today is a result of their love, support, grace, and teaching.

I bounced around a bit before I settled back at my boyhood location. Married now, with two daughters of my own, it's interesting how perspective changes. I find myself looking through a different lens at the same life. Instead of seeking adventure and pushing life to the max, I look at the blessed responsibility of being a husband and a father. Before marriage and children, it was hard for me to understand what would be asked of me, but after holding our first baby girl in my arms at the hospital for the first time, all presumptions and priorities were attuned. All I thought I knew was about to be tested. Looking in to the eyes of our newborn and feeling the weight of responsibility for what unspoken needs would be required of me was a defining experience. "Train a child in the way he should go and when he is old he will not stray from it" (Proverbs 22:6). I am so thankful that this is truth, and I am thankful that my parents had the patience and fortitude to raise five sons as their primary job and not a second hand approach. I am thankful because as my girls grow up each day, I never really know what kind of job I am doing. All I know is what I was taught by Mom and Dad and how that applies to my family. There were not enough books to prepare me for the realities of marriage or fatherhood, but what I was taught, even from the early age of throwing cantaloupes down stairs, is what I fall back on: when you make a mess, you have to clean it up (no, that is really not the take away here, it just fit).

One of the biggest and most impactful lessons I was taught by my family stuck with me: if it's in the Word, it is truth, because the Word is Truth. So if I aim to train my child in the way he should go and trust that when he is old he will not stray from it, and strive to love my wife as Christ loved the Church, then I trust that the Holy Spirit will order my steps.

BURT SR.

Burt Sr. And Careen

Here I was a bachelor for 33 years, about to marry a godly Christian girl, Careen Hart, on July 19, 1969. That was to be a life-changing experience. We were both only children, about to embark on a life of parenting five boys with no training, no understanding of the responsibilities, or godly wisdom. The previous 20 years were characterized by a selfish and egotistical, fleshly life. With my parents, I had regularly attended a small country Methodist church since childhood, hardly ever missing a service. Although I held the position of president of the Youth Group and later held other church offices, I had little understanding of salvation. I was without Jesus as Savior and Lord. I made a change when I got to college: I never went to church.

In the second year of our marriage, Careen and I attended a non-denominational, ecumenical conference in Atlanta. My agreement to go was the result of much prayer from my wife and both of our parents. As part of my farming operation, I was growing crops for a large freezing plant at the time. Weather conditions were volatile, and I saw no way I could leave to attend the conference. My willingness to go was predicated on having perfect weather for completing the harvest on schedule. It was no surprise to God, but amazing to me, that everything worked to perfection.

The second night of the conference, I found myself walking down the isle, following the tug in my heart that later I knew was the Holy Spirit. When the Catholic Bishop who was the speaker that night came to pray for me, he asked, "What do you want?" I said, "I want everything God has for me." At that moment I met Jesus as my Savior and was baptized in His Holy Spirit. When we came home, we started meeting with four other couples for a weekly Bible study, which lasted over four years. Together, we explored God's word. Certain Scriptures took residence in our hearts, and formed the foundation for our marriage and parenting adventure.

Concerning our marriage, Ephesians 5:25 challenged me as a husband by saying, "Husbands, love your wife just as Christ loved the church and gave himself for her," and that I was to nourish and cherish Careen as my own body. I was bewildered by this command until I discovered in later years that Jesus prayed in John 17:26, "Father, give them the same love that we have for each other." I came to realize this love is only possible when we cleanse our own temple (our own self) and become prepared for His indwelling.

Concerning my role as a father, there were several very convicting Scriptures. Deuteronomy 6:5-9 (NKJV), "You shall love the Lord your God with all your heart, with all your soul, and with all your strength. And these words which I command shall be in your heart, and you shall teach them diligently to your children. You shall talk of them as you sit in your house, when you walk by the way, when you lie down, and when you rise up. You shall bind them as a sign on your hand, and they shall be as frontlets between your eyes, and you shall write them on the doorposts of your house and on your gates."

As a fledgling father, there were times that I didn't have the wisdom of God, particularly in how to respond to a conflict between sons. With the clumsiness that comes with doing things apart from God's leading, I entered the conflict. At a time like this, I said to Careen, "I messed that up, didn't I?" to which she responded, "Yep. You blew it."

I didn't realize the effect a spontaneous angry response had on one of our sons until years after the particular event. A group of fathers and sons were mingling in our front yard, enjoying the camaraderie, when one of my sons playfully knocked off my cap. Being sensitive to my thinning hair, I overreacted by scolding him. I had no idea the wound I caused at that time would stay with him until twenty years later he brought up the incident and confessed to me how devastated he felt when I humiliated him in front of his friends. He had trusted our relationship to be deeper than that. I cried and asked his forgiveness, and the hurt was amended.

Then there were times when I received an audible from the Holy Spirit. One such time, I reacted when one of our boys pushed me beyond my ability to handle my emotions. I had just come in hot and wet with sweat from the field and not in the mood for a long discussion. When our son gave me an evasive answer to a question, anger rose in me like nothing I'd experienced. I was about to hit him when I heard a voice that seemed to come from above and behind my right shoulder. With calm and loving authority, the Voice said, "Don't. Do. That." Time seemed to stand still. My anger instantly vanished, I released my hold on his shirt, and I said, "Forgive me, Son. I will never do that again." That moment of having a repentant heart and asking my son's forgiveness had an effect on me that I've never forgotten. Even when provoked, the memory of that Voice has never let me reach such pivotal anger again.

Over the years, I have come to this conclusion. In Hebrews 12:2, the writer refers to the race that Jesus had set before Him, and the joy He anticipated when it was over. I apply this verse to the charge set before us. We have to endure the trials and challenges of marriage and parenting, and we too can set our hearts on pleasing God and experience the joy that comes with staying the course. One day I will stand before the Father, knowing that I am accountable to Him for the responsibility He gave me through His Word when He said in Psalm 78: 5-7 (NKJV),

> For He established a testimony in Jacob, and He appointed a law in Israel, which He commanded our fathers, that they should make them known to their children; that the generation to come might know them, the children who would be born. That they may arise and declare them to their children, that they may set their hope in God, and not forget the works of God, but keep His commandments.

Looking at where we are at this season of our lives, Careen and I are seeing the fruit of the Spirit developing between us and among our family members. We are experiencing a deepening awareness of God's presence operating in us, and we see the days of our lives characterized by more love—more patience, more tenderness, more thoughtfulness, more caring—for one another. We start our day excited about the opportunities God puts before us. We thrive in knowing He has a purpose in our lives, and we're grateful for the blessing of being able to invest in the next generation. We rejoice in the promise He gave us in Psalm 92:13-15 (NKJV),

Those who are planted in the house of the Lord shall flourish in the courts of our God. They shall still bear fruit in old age; they shall be fresh and flourishing, to declare that the Lord is upright; He is my rock, and there is no unrighteousness in Him.

THANKS AND CREDITS

I want to thank some wonderful people for the help and encouragement for this project. First, thank you, Gloria Graham, for your willingness to read and reread the manuscript and help me express myself. I hope one day to meet you personally.

Thank you, Young Women, who have honored me by asking my advice and opinion, and have shared the needs of your heart with me — especially the Tuesday Morning Mamas. Thank you, Young Moms, who responded to my questionnaire and expressed the concerns of your heart. I applaud all of you for your dedication to your families and to rearing godly children.

Thank you, my special Christian sisters, Gaile and Joan, for your encouragement to me in this project.

Thank you, Amber, for your assistance with my technological challenges, for your tolerance in listening to my ideas, for your practical and insightful advice...and for babysitting our grandchildren!

Thank you, Family, for your overwhelming support. I never dreamed you guys would take this as seriously as you have, and I am deeply grateful...and humbled. Thank you for the witnesses that you are, and for living lives that validate everything I've said here. Without your Curtain Calls, this story would have been incomplete. It amazes me (but doesn't surprise me) that your contributions are so similar — and none of you knew what the others had written!

Thank you for vying to be my favorite. You're all right: you are.

Thank you, sweet Daughters-in-law, for being the daughters I never had, for loving our sons, and together with them, establishing homes that honor the Lord. We couldn't ask for more perfect mothers for our grandchildren.

Thank you, my Husband, for playing the lead role, yet making me look like the star.

Finally, thank You, Father God, for bestowing on me the honor of mothering five of Your sons. I am eternally grateful you deemed me worthy for the task.

Growing Family

ENDNOTES

1   Pat King, *How Do You Find the Time?* (Tacoma, WA: Aglow Publishing, 1995), 10.
2   Nancy Leigh DeMoss, *A Place of Quiet Rest* (Chicago, IL: Moody Press, 2000), 42,44.
3   Chuck Swindoll, *Parenting: From Surviving to Thriving* (Nashville, TN: W. Publishing Group, 2006).
4   Florence Littauer, *Personality Plus for Parents* (Grand Rapids, MI: Fleming H. Revell, 2000), 8.
5   Susanna Wesley, quoted on *Hannah's Reflections* blog, April 21, 2009.
6   John Eldredge, *Wild at Heart* (Nashville, TN: Thomas Nelson, 2011).
7   Dale Carnegie, *How to win Friends and Influence People* (USA: Simon and Schuster, 1963).
8   Dr. Bill Ligon, *Imparting the Blessing Handbook* (Brunswick, GA: The Father's Blessing, 2013).